MW01009423

RIDING WITH STRANGERS

A HITCHHIKER'S JOURNEY

ELIJAH WALD

CHICAGO
REVIEW
PRESS

Library of Congress Cataloging-in-Publication Data

Wald, Elijah.

   Riding with strangers : a hitchhiker's journey / Elijah Wald.

      p. cm.

   ISBN 1-55652-605-9

   1. United States—Description and travel.   2. United States—
Social life and customs—1971–   3. Wald, Elijah—Travel—United
States.   I. Title.

   E169.Z83W348   2006

   917.304'931—dc22   2005028296

Cover design: Rachel McClain
Interior design: Pamela Juárez

Published by Chicago Review Press, Incorporated
814 North Franklin Street
Chicago, Illinois 60610
ISBN-13: 978-1-55652-605-3
ISBN 10: 1-55652-605-9
Printed in the United States of America
5 4 3 2 1

To Sandrine, who always picks me up

أوتو ستوب (auto-stop)	Arabic (North African)
搭便車 (bian)	Chinese (Mandarin)
cestovat stopem, jet stopem	Czech
liften	Dutch
faire du stop	French
trampen; per Anhalter fahren	German
κάνω ώτοστοπ (kano otostop)	Greek
לתפוס טרמפ (litfos tremp)	Hebrew
stoppol	Hungarian
membonceng	Indonesian
ヒッチハイク (hicchihaiku)	Japanese
히치하이크 (hich'ihaik'ŭ)	Korean
haere paoeke	Maori
andar à boleia	Portuguese
ИДТИ АВТОСТОПОМ (idti avtostopom)	Russian
hacer dedo	Spanish (Castilian)
ir en raid, ir en aventon	Spanish (Mexican)
kupakiwa-njiani	Swahili
otostop yapmak	Turkish
Đi nhờ xe	Vietnamese

My proposal is: To set off walking this afternoon. To stop when we are tired. To get a lift when we can. To walk when we can't. To do it at once, and do it cheap.

—**Charles Dickens, *Martin Chuzzlewit***

"Damn," said I, "I'll just hitchhike on that highway . . ."

—**Jack Kerouac, "Good Blonde"**

Auto, Auto, may I have a ride?
Yes, sir. Yes, sir. Step right inside.

—**Nursery rhyme**

Reagan . . . stood on the corner of routes 26 and 29 in Ohio while thumbing a ride to Dixon.

—**Ronald Reagan Birthplace Web site**

Bobbie thumbed a diesel down, just before it rained,
Took us all the way to New Orleans.

—**Kris Kristofferson, "Me and Bobbie McGee"**

Dear Mom, I've hitchhiked to San Francisco.
Don't be mad.

—**Janis Joplin**

I'm gonna find that girl if I have to hitchhike around the world.

—**Marvin Gaye, "Hitch Hike"**

On the second day, a sail drew near, nearer, and picked me up at last.

—**Herman Melville, *Moby-Dick***

lot of people who are very different from you, and with whom you might disagree about almost everything, are being awfully nice to you. It is an education I would recommend to any young person, and plenty of old ones too.

And yet, as is obvious to anyone cruising the highways, the roadside is no longer thick with optimistic voyagers, eager to run away from home and explore the wide open spaces. The romance of hitchhiking is largely forgotten or dismissed, except in the nostalgic memories of graying bohemians reminiscing about their long-departed youth. Put the contemporary American subconscious on the couch and ask it to say the first thing that comes to mind when it hears the word "hitchhiking," and the most likely response will be "dangerous."

That's why I'm out here on this rainy September morning, waiting for a ride. I am headed for the Pacific Northwest, but the destination hardly matters. In the last few years, while I've hitched in Mexico, in France, in Spain—even briefly in Texas and Arizona—I haven't done a proper, cross-country jaunt, and my cheerful proselytizing is meeting with ever more dubious responses. People tell me I'm living in the past, in a safer, friendlier world that bears little resemblance to today's highways. I respond that in my experience people are pretty decent and helpful, and that the world is by no means as dangerous a place as you would think from watching television or reading the newspapers.

These are hard times for a lot of people, in America and around the world, but the most dangerous thing we can do is to distrust the basic decency of the folks we meet every day. Because the most serious threats to our well-being rarely come from our neighbors, even in the worst neighborhoods. On the contrary, the greatest danger is that we will isolate ourselves in cocoons of mistrust, unable to get together with others who share common needs and interests because we feel so threatened and alone. There is a phrase that has always stuck with me, though its source is long forgotten: "If you trust everyone you meet, you will occasionally get robbed; but if you distrust everyone, you will spend your whole life surrounded by thieves."

So I have a mission: to demonstrate that it remains reasonably safe to get out on the road and look for rides, and that, despite all the horror stories in the news, there are still plenty of people who are happy to pull over and invite an unknown wanderer into their cars.

Beyond that, I want to give some tips to anyone who cares to follow my example, and a taste of the experience for the armchair traveler—not of the exceptional, weird rides, but of the normal experience of a hitch across the country. And also, for what it's worth, to give some sense of what I love about it, which may be hardest of all. It is an unusual taste, and I cannot help noticing that even my old hitchhiking buddies have taken up other modes of transportation. And yet, it still seems to me a uniquely pleasurable form of travel, one that introduced me to thousands of people I otherwise would never have met, and taught me immeasurable lessons about the world around me.

A DEFENSE OF THE GENTLE
ART OF HITCHHIKING

Despite the calumnies leveled at it by ignorant and conservative critics, hitchhiking has as noble a heritage as any means of travel on earth. Consider a few examples.

We are all born hitchhikers: for the months until we learn to crawl, we can travel only when some decent soul, for no pay but the pleasure of our company, chooses to pick us up.

When proud Odysseus was cast on Phaeacia's shores, and only for the beauty of his countenance and his nobility of bearing was taken in and carried by ship to Ithaca, what was he but a hitchhiker?

Likewise Sinbad the Sailor, who setting forth each voyage a rich merchant was oft-times forced to stand at length on some strange strand and hitch a vessel home to Baghdad.

How many castaways, famous or unknown, have chosen to do likewise? And how many tired ramblers on how many dusty roads have been taken up by kindly wagoners?

Would some say, granting all of that, that hitchhiking is a mere act of desperation or begging, and has no special virtue? Recall the patron saint of travelers, Saint Christopher—who was he but someone who gave a lift to a hitchhiker, and who was that hitchhiker but the infant Jesus?

Or, if you prefer the Old Testament: when Jonah fled in fear from the Lord, he did it as a registered passenger, taking a berth on a ship and paying his fare—but when he repented of his cowardice, he hitched a ride with a passing whale.

Is this not good company? And there are hundreds more who could be added to the list. But more of that later. First let us look deeper into the whys and wherefores of the art, and then get out on the road and see for ourselves.

SOUND AND FURY

Why hitchhike? As well ask: Why set out on any adventure? It is not the most predictable or secure form of travel, the one you would select when you had a pressing engagement or a prescribed round of appointments. But when you have the time and inclination to wander for a while through unknown climes, open to whatever they may hold, there is no better means.

Hitchhiking combines the greatest pleasures of travel, and raises them to their highest plane. There is freedom, first of all, the liberty to go where you will, to escape your workaday responsibilities, and, above all, to liberate yourself from the stocks in which friendly expectation locks and hobbles your homebound character. Among our friends, we must be ourselves with all our history, known for what our common, daily habits have made us. Out in the world, we can reinvent ourselves at every turn. And what better theater for this reinvention than the shifting stages of cars, trucks, and vans, each driven by a different and hospitable chauffeur? We enter their world already a romantic character, the lone wanderer, the man or woman without a country. We can choose to play a variation on this part or to play against it, to fulfill the myth or to reassure the drivers of our ordinariness and familiarity. In either case, there is no past or future to be overcome. We sit our hour or more on the passenger seat, and then that act is done and intermission taken by the roadside, until the next set comes rolling up and the plot adds a new twist.

And there you have the second pleasure: surprise. What would be the point of travel if we knew precisely what awaited us? The excitement comes from facing the unknown, experiencing new things and testing how they suit and work upon our humors. Traveling by train or bus, or worst of all by plane, we have subtracted the journey itself from this equation. If we fly to Guatemala, we may be astonished, enlightened, and edified by what we find on arrival, but we have experienced nothing in the intervening miles that would not have been identical en route to Dresden, Dakar, or Detroit. A bus or train is somewhat more in tune with its environment, but nonetheless that environment unfolds only through the window, watched as in a movie, while we remain cocooned in the mass-produced and proudly unvaried sameness of Greyhound or Amtrak. How many of us even talk to our fellow passengers? And how many of them would appreciate the intrusion? We are all marking time in a traveling antechamber, waiting for the doors to open on our chosen destination.

Of course there are those who, seeking freedom, set out in their own cars, their own hands on the wheel, individual masters of their destinies. It's the great American road trip: the lone driver, or better yet a pair of drivers—Jack and Neal, Thelma and Louise, Bonnie and Clyde. But that myth carries its own counterspell: to the extent that we keep to our own conveyance, it is our jail as well as our chariot. We ride like the tortoise, imprisoned in our cozy shell, even if we drive from Nome to Patagonia. This is the marketable fantasy of contemporary travel: the pleasures of adventure with all the comforts of home. While cultured travelers sneer at the package tourists who want to have their pizza, hamburgers, and deep-fried chicken instantly available wherever they may wander, how far is that from all the other, subtler means we employ to carry our own worlds along with us? How can we show greater contempt for the magic of a foreign place than to touch it only when and if we choose?

Poets, philosophers, and sociologists bemoan the isolation that has been a side effect of virtually all progress and invention since the Industrial Revolution. Machines have brought us many advantages, but also have inexorably cut us off from the day-to-day intercourse that once was an inescapable part of life. Read any older travel narrative and it will be full of tales of strangers met by chance on the road, sharing a little time and a few experiences, companions until the next city and as much a part of the countryside as the trees and farmhouses. Walking along foreign roads, earlier pilgrims were always in the company of native guides who could steer them to a friendly inn or fill them with the latest gossip, then point the way over the next mountain. Today, that experience has all but disappeared. I once tried to recapture the feel of a medieval journey by walking across northern France. It was excellent exercise, but I have rarely been more alone. Though the French were all around me, they whizzed by in their cars and I met with barely a half dozen people in my monthlong trek.

Contrast that experience with a day's hitchhiking: Anywhere in the world, you get into a car and you meet with a companion. Often the driver is acquainted with the region and can point out sights or suggest diversions, but more to the point, he or she becomes part of your experience, an unbreakable human link to those particular miles. You travel with the natives, and are treated as a guest and introduced to cultures and homes that otherwise would remain silent and shut.

It is people who make our world, for better or worse. Writers have often hymned the glories of unpeopled nature, but that is for a rest, not a lifetime. We are soothed and edified by Wordsworth's evocation of a solitary lakeside or Edward Abbey's of a trackless desert, but we read to be companions of the writers, not to duplicate their solitude. It may give us joy to walk alone in nature for a few hours, or even for a day or two—but good company can keep us fascinated for hours, days, weeks, and years. And when it comes to travel, it is people that make foreign lands foreign and the exotic exotic. What would be the thrill of going to Quito, Athens, or Beijing if the people there were just the same as those we left at home? Why else is Japan more foreign to a New Englander than the Arizona desert, or Egypt more foreign to an Arizonan than the glaciers of Montana? And as a means of traveling among people, hitchhiking has no peer.

I came of age in a time when the love of hitchhiking and humanity was commonplace. The roads were full of college students, hippies, Kerouac-mad poets, Guthrie-mad guitarists, as well as hoboes, tramps, and young adventurers of the sort that have taken to the road since time immemorial. If you saw a musician on a street corner, or a charcoal portraitist, or a couple just arrived in town with backpacks and tired expressions, you didn't have to ask how they got there. We all hitched, and as a general thing our parents had hitched before us—even the most respectable of them, on vacations from school, as adults grounded by wartime gas rationing, or simply because they needed to get to the next town and did not care to wait for a bus. It was considered a slow and haphazard means of travel, but enlivened by interesting experiences and quaint and colorful characters.

Today, the roadsides are empty. We see advertisements for "adventure travel," but almost always the adventure is in nature— scaling the peaks of the Himalayas, trekking the Alaskan tundra, or penetrating the jungles of the Amazon, with hired guides and all the latest equipment. Sensible people would rather trust their fortunes to a thin rope on a slick glacier, or the flimsy wings of a hang glider, than to the goodwill of an unknown driver. Tell your friends that you intend to hitchhike from coast to coast, and you will inevitably hear the same two echoing refrains: "No one will stop for you," and "You could do that in the sixties, but it's much too dangerous these days." No evidence is ever introduced for these assertions, but they are the common currency of the interchange, tendered as if backed up by a Fort Knox of statistics and investigative reportage.

This ubiquitous nay-saying is symptomatic of the paranoia that bedevils Americans and is a tragedy of our time—and yet, it has its good side: With the roadsides empty there is no competition, and the hitchhiking is better than ever.

SERVICE PLAZA

So there I was, standing in the rain on the first service plaza outside Boston, sticking my thumb out whenever a car passed. It was not the most romantic spot, but you have to start somewhere. Service areas are easy, efficient places to pick up rides, especially on a toll highway like the Massachusetts Turnpike. Left to their own devices, drivers stop for gas, food, or bathrooms whenever they feel the need or inclination, but on toll roads they only get an opportunity every thirty miles or so. As a result, service areas provide the hitchhiker's equivalent of a captive audience, and if the weather gets nasty you can go into the restaurant for a cup of coffee, or stand by the doors and approach drivers directly. But redolent of freedom and adventure they are not. They are bland and prefabricated, full of brand-name fast foods, clean restrooms, plastic souvenirs, all pressed like interchangeable widgets from the same mold, coast to coast and border to border.

My current service area was laid out in the standard pattern: driving in, signs directed cars left and trucks right, the former to the neatly laid-out lot around the entrance of the restaurant, the latter to the sprawling expanse behind the building. Casual motorists get the benefit of bright signs and a bit of lawn, and their gas pumps are always beyond the restaurant, since they must be enticed to spend a little extra money on their way through. Truckers get a utilitarian lot and their pumps are generally alongside the building; they stop for gas so infrequently, and the fueling takes so long, that they need no urging to buy some food or coffee, and maybe take a shower while they're at it. On this particular plaza, an island of concrete extended beyond the building to the pump area, after which it turned to grass and narrowed to a point where cars and trucks converged, channeled into a single lane leading back onto the highway. Before that point, a hitchhiker would have to choose between cars or trucks. After that point, the only place to stand would be on the exit ramp itself, where drivers were already trying to get up speed and legal complications might ensue—pedestrians are forbidden on the interstate in most states, including all the ones east of the Mississippi.

I stood on the grassy point, in the gray drizzle, holding a purple umbrella over my head. A silly enough spectacle, I am sure, but not in any way threatening. Who has ever been mugged by a clean-cut, neatly dressed man with a guitar and a purple umbrella? I had a poncho in my pack, but a poncho covers you completely and makes it hard for drivers to get a sense of how you look, and the more fastidious also worry that you will get their car wet if they let you inside. Hence the umbrella. My guitar was wrapped in a green plastic leaf bag, twisted so as to make the shape of the instrument as obvious as possible. Except in southern Europe, where it is occasionally mistaken for a large smoked ham, the shape of a guitar is pretty recognizable—and in any case it doesn't look like a potential weapon.

There I stood from nine fifteen to ten fifteen, on that little peninsula of wet grass. My pack was tilted against a signpost, as visible as possible, to show that I was a serious traveler. The guitar rested on my foot, to keep it off the wet ground, plastic bag notwithstanding, supported by one hand when I was not hitching and leaning against my waist when I reached out to thumb, since my other hand held the umbrella. Since the cars passed on my right and the trucks on my left, this involved a certain amount of switching back and forth—not that the truck drivers would fail to notice me if I didn't have a thumb out on their side, but it is always good policy to hitch each driver directly, meet his or her eyes, and try to establish some sort of communication. If you are doing it right, they will at least acknowledge you with an apologetic smile, a gesture, a shake of the head. Even if they just look annoyed or give a thumbs-down sign, you are still making contact. As long as people can't ignore you, one will eventually decide to stop.

Such were the thoughts with which I cheered myself as I stood there for an hour in the rain. One trucker did pull over—a Sikh, with a long, pointed beard, a white turban, and precise, Indian diction—but only to explain that although he personally would be happy to take me, his company had very strict rules against carrying passengers. Not a ride, but friendly, and thus encouraging. I was prepared for a longer wait than usual, because this was the first rest area out of Boston and relatively few of the drivers passing me would be going any serious distance. Leaving a city is always harder than getting a ride in mid-journey. And rain doesn't help. Not only will drivers worry about your getting their seats wet, but the weather affects their general mood. People tend to feel helpful and hospitable when they are feeling cheerful about life. Sunny days make for fine hitchhiking, as does light traffic. Rain and rush hours make drivers sullen and impatient, and the result is predictable for anyone dependent on their good will. (The only exception I have found to this rule is in Norway, where drivers instantly pull over at the first drops of rain. I don't know why they are an exception, but it made me very fond of Norway.) All in all, I could make plenty of excuses for the cars that were passing me by, and in any case I was enjoying the feeling of being out on the road for the first time in several months. I was eager to get a ride, but it was not a bad hour.

Then the cop pulled over.

COP

I saw him coming, of course. All I was doing was watching the approaching traffic, and I spotted the police markings as soon as he turned off the highway. I didn't hitch him as he neared my spot, but neither did I worry much. I have never had any trouble from police when I was on a rest area, though they have often shooed me back onto one when I drifted too far down the exit ramp.

He stopped alongside me and rolled down his passenger window. He was maybe thirty years old, with dark blond hair in a crew cut. Calm and professional: "Where are you going?"

"Cleveland." It was a tactically balanced response: far enough away for me to be serious about getting there and for it to be a relatively pricey bus ticket, but not so far that I would seem like an out-and-out tramp.

"Cleveland! Where are you coming from?"

"Boston."

"Can I see some ID?"

"Of course." I reached for my back pocket, where my wallet was, while he continued the interrogation.

"Did you know that it's an arrestable offense to hitchhike out here on the interstate?"

"No, sir. I thought it was OK on the rest areas."

"Have you ever been arrested?"

"No sir, and I'm giving you my ID, so you can check that out." By now I had my driver's license out, and I handed it to him. He looked it over, wrote something down on a yellow pad, but didn't call it in.

"So what are you planning on doing now?"

"I was hoping to get to Ohio by tonight."

"Do you know people in Boston?"

"Sure. I grew up here."

"Well, you're gonna have to go over to that restaurant and call someone to come out and get you, or call a taxi, because you can't stay out here. This is all part of the interstate, and the law is that you cannot solicit rides here. You know, the law is for your own safety. There are a lot of crazy people out there. Those truck drivers, a lot of them are predators. It's not like you see in the movies."

OK, so it was going to be like that. "I understand, sir. But you know, I've been doing this for a lot of years. I'm in my forties, and I've been doing this since I was in my teens."

"Well, if you're in your forties, maybe it's time you thought about quitting. Things change, you know. It's not like it used to be. There are a lot of knifings, people get robbed and killed."

"Like I said, I've been doing this a long time, and so far I've been lucky . . ."

"I'm glad you understand that it's been luck. Not everybody has been lucky. A lot of hitchhikers have been hurt, and a lot of drivers have been hurt. So some laws got made, for everybody's protection. I know it used to be different, but things change. It's not as free a country as it used to be."

That one stopped me for a moment, but it also looked like an opening. "Excuse me for saying this, sir, but you said that, not me . . ."

He handed me back my license.

"OK, listen: You have to go in there and call someone to come get you. If any other officer comes through and sees you out here, you could get arrested." I was nodding, the requisite acquiescence. "Now, I'm going to drive off, and I won't be back through here for at least a few hours. Do you understand what I'm saying to you?"

"Yes sir, I understand completely."

He drove off, down the ramp and onto the highway, and I waited politely until he was out of sight. Then I turned around and went back to hitching.

LAWS OF THE HIGHWAY

Lawmen and vagabonds. Cops and adventurers. Highway patrolmen and knights of the road. It's an odd relationship. With few exceptions, I have been treated well by the police when they have found me on the roadside, but I'm always aware that if I happen to meet an officer who had a bad egg for breakfast he can take it out on me. I keep to my best behavior, watching for signals, adjusting my accent, avoiding any comment that might irritate him. (Or her, of course. I've never been pulled over by a highway patrolwoman, but there are a few out there.)

Hitchhiking is illegal on many roads—on all roads in a few states—and even where legal it is always a borderline activity. Going west on the interstates, it is thoroughly prohibited until one hits Iowa, and then allowed or not in a state-by-state patchwork. I say "allowed" rather than legal, because the laws and their enforcement are two quite different things. Like the signs forbidding singing in Irish pubs, the hitchhiking laws in a lot of states are there to give the police an excuse to bust people they feel like busting, but they are not enforced in normal practice—especially not on neatly dressed white people. Even where enforcement is more general, a well-placed "Yes sir" every couple of sentences can keep you on the road, or at least delay your ejection.

I recall a long evening trying to leave Chicago: I had been standing for a couple of hours just past the tollbooth on I-90, a wait made memorable by the moment when a truck pulled over in front of me, the driver climbed down from his cab, walked over to me, and said, "I just got home from ten days on the road. I live down the road there, about thirty miles back. I come home, and there's a note there on the counter from my wife. She's left out of there, says she doesn't want to live with me anymore, and she's gone off with my best friend. I just walked out the door again and got back in the truck and started driving. I had to tell somebody that." Then he walked back to his truck, climbed in, and drove off.

Anyway, after I had been standing there for a couple of hours, an Illinois state trooper pulled over and told me it was illegal to hitch on the interstate. I expressed surprise, as is appropriate in such situations, and asked what I should do. He wrote out a ticket, telling me that this time he wouldn't fine me, but he was giving me a warning. As to what I should do, that was kind of a problem. If I climbed over the fence to the field beside the road, I would be trespassing on private property, and in any case I was several miles from the nearest entrance ramp, where hitching was legal.

(I was glad he saw things that way; a pair of Swiss cops, faced with a similar dilemma, once forced me to climb a fence and walk along it for a mile to a bridge across the highway, then another mile back to where I could stand at the head of an entrance ramp. They had found me at the foot of this same ramp, but since it was technically part of the highway they could not permit me to simply walk up it, and the officious bastards actually sat in their car and watched me until I reached the bridge. American cops, whatever their faults, do not waste that sort of time and energy holding minor offenders to the letter of the law.) The Illinois trooper's solution was to tell me that he would drive off and let me stay there, but I had better take the first ride that would get me into Indiana.

"Is it legal to hitch on the interstate there?" I asked.

"No, they have the same law we do. But they don't enforce theirs." A subtle distinction, especially in this case. He then explained that he could not give me the warning he had written, because if another officer came by and found it on my person, they would know he had warned me and let me stay.

As at today's service plaza, that cop was white, I was white, and I was clean and carrying a guitar and backpack. I have no idea how either situation would have turned out had I been black or had an accent, or a beard, or been more obviously poor, or been female. Or had it been a different cop, or a different day. So I'll just say that I was lucky both times, and a few others as well. And that the laws on the books provide only a vague guide to what any particular cop is going to do in a particular situation. And that, whatever they may say, the cops know as well as I do that hitchhiking is a lot less dangerous than the official picture might suggest.

Indeed, I am not aware of any relationship between the genuine dangers of hitchhiking and the enforcement of hitchhiking laws. Whatever the cops or legislators may say, the choice to prohibit hitching is like the choice to prohibit loitering, or begging, or sleeping in the park. It is not about safety, it is about creating an atmosphere of order and control. Some studies have suggested that creating this atmosphere cuts down on crime. Very likely, on the more disorderly kinds of crime, the crimes of poor people who have no choice but to commit them in public places rather than offices. But, like so many of the pleasures of life, both the choice to hitchhike and the choice to pick up hitchhikers are based on the assumption that there are more precious things than safety, and that those things may be lost if we give way to paranoia—and the country becomes less free than it used to be.

DANGERS

As I told the officer, I have been lucky, and despite years of dire warnings have rarely felt I was in any danger while hitchhiking—or, more precisely, have rarely felt I was the focus of any threat. The most common danger to hitchhikers is the danger shared by everyone who makes the choice to hurtle down a highway protected only by a thin wall of metal and a nylon strap: not robbers, sex fiends, or axe murderers, but drunk or careless drivers. For example, the ride that finally took me into Indiana after my meeting with the Illinois statie was with a wild-eyed guy in a party mood, passing a bottle back and forth with his friend in the shotgun seat while careening down the interstate like a Chinese ribbon dancer, bouncing on the shoulder and occasionally kissing the cement center barrier. He was going all the way to Ohio, but once we were safely past Gary I made my excuses and spent the night curled up on the grass by a suburban exit ramp.

I have been robbed only once while hitching, and even then it was not by a driver. I was standing on the road out of Windhoek, Namibia, and some young guys wandered over and asked about my guitar. I played them a tune, and then one of them asked if he could try it. He strummed a few chords with his friends crowding around, then jumped the fence by the highway while two of his pals grabbed my pack. I don't remember all the details—things were happening pretty quickly—but there was a moment when I was rolling in a ditch with one of them, and then I was standing with my arms held behind me and a screwdriver at my throat. Then they took off into the hills by the road, and I followed along behind them, which was easy because they were trying to carry my pack between two of them and that slowed them down. One guy threw a couple of rocks at me, but after a minute they dropped the pack and ran off with the guitar, which was what they really wanted. Music lovers are everywhere. Only after it was all over did I consider the odd fact that, although there were five of them and I was alone, and we were up on the mountainside where no one could interfere, they never tried to hurt me. Even when we were rolling in the ditch, neither I nor the other guy threw a punch; we were just wrestling, as if we were kids in a schoolyard. I was sorry to lose the guitar, of course, but even that had its good side: I had to hitch back to South Africa to buy another, and was picked up by a biologist from a field station in the desert, who asked me if I was in a hurry and, when I replied in the negative, proceeded to navigate most of the way on dirt roads through the dunes, occasionally stopping to take me on an expertly narrated nature walk.

I suppose I would have felt very differently about that robbery if it had happened at the beginning of my travels, but it didn't. By the time I hit Namibia, I had been hitchhiking for over a dozen years, on four continents, so I could take comfort in the tens of thousands of miles already covered without a hint of assault. In that way, hitchhiking is sort of like living in a dodgy neighborhood: if you get mugged the week you move in, you might move right out again, but if you've been living there happily for a long time, one robbery doesn't define the place for you.

Obviously, hitching is safer if you are male, and still more if you are an older, relatively experienced-looking male. When I was eighteen or twenty, although I was never threatened, I had my share of cruising creeps. The first time I ever hitched alone, I was headed out of Zaragoza, Spain, and was picked up by a soft, pudgy guy with thick glasses and acne scars who tried to grope me, then dumped me in the desert. It was like a B movie: as he drove off, a tumbleweed rolled by, and I realized that there was no water or human habitation in sight and that I had left that morning without eating or drinking anything. Trained by Hollywood to know the proper behavior in such circumstances, I immediately began dying of thirst. I trudged down the road, my throat parched and my tongue thickening. An occasional car passed, paying me no mind. It was brutally hot, and the road ahead shimmered, taunting me with mirages of water. After a couple of hours, I passed a shady patch of dirt where tire tracks held a puddle of muddy moisture. Ignoring everything my mother told me, I fell to my knees and wet my cracking lips. Slightly revived, I walked on and, topping the next rise, saw a gas station in the distance. It took another half hour to get there, but they had some stale rolls and a refrigerator of drinks. I ate a roll, drank half a bottle of milk, walked back to the roadside, and the first car that passed was a family on their way home from vacation who took me all the way to Madrid. Trials overcome and virtue rewarded.

I was eighteen, and never for a moment unaware that it would make a good story.

Other times, the annoyances have come without any cinematic trappings. I once hitched out of San Francisco and had five drivers in a row pick me up, proposition me, then drop me at the next exit. Only one bothered to drive me to an intersection where there was a decent flow of traffic; he was also the only one who offered to pay me. I was apparently a good deal prettier in those days. It has been more than ten years since a driver put his hand on my leg or passed me a porn magazine to see my reaction. So when people suggest that I am getting too old to hitchhike, I note the advantages.

Even when I was young and attractive, I never found any of my would-be seducers to be more than a passing annoyance. Had I been a young woman, I might have felt differently about these incidents. Then again, I have met young women hitchhiking alone—more in Europe than in the United States, but over here as well. Driving through North Dakota with my ex-half-sister-in-law, Hazel, we picked up a slight, pretty French Canadian on her way home to Quebec after hitching down to Texas and over to the West Coast. I'm sure she was tired of hearing the question, but I asked if she had run into any tricky situations, and she said her experiences had been about like mine: men sometimes made passes, but had always taken no for an answer. In her case, they had actually tended to be more chivalrous, taking her on to her destination rather than promptly pulling over and leaving her by the road. And just a couple of years ago, driving a rental car out of Davis, California, late in the evening, I picked up a young Asian woman en route from Los Angeles to San Francisco. I asked her if she wasn't scared to be hitching, especially at night, and she explained that she was a Christian and God was watching over her. She had gotten a ride from L.A. to Sacramento in a truck, and from there to Davis in another, and said she had made the trip many times.

Most women, though, prefer to hitch with a companion, and more often than not a male companion. Or at least most of the women I have seen on the road—which may be quite another matter. There are plenty of hitchhikers who arrange their rides at rest areas or truck stops, approaching drivers directly, and they are invisible to passing cars. If a woman cared to hitch with the bare minimum of risk, she could travel rest area to rest area and never even speak to a male driver. In any case, a single woman tends to get rides so fast that the chances of seeing one standing on the road are minimal. Being less threatening, women or couples get a lot of rides that would sensibly pass me by.

Because, of course, the people who stop for us are also subject to dangers. Like the threat to hitchhikers, the threat to drivers is much exaggerated, but right around the time of my last cross-country trip a crazed hitchhiker killed two drivers in Massachusetts and one in New Hampshire. So yes, hitchhiking has some genuine perils—but they are awfully rare compared to its pleasures. It is the nature of hitchhiking to be based on vulnerability and trust, and ruled by chance. The robber or rapist who elected hitching as a way of accosting his victims would be an odd assailant indeed—he could find likelier prey on any city street. So the crimes of hitchhikers are few, and though they are no less real for that, reality has little to do with why so many cars pass us by.

The real danger involved in picking up a hitchhiker is that he or she will interfere with the pleasures of the drive. Americans, more than any other people on earth, see their cars as extensions of themselves, steel suits they put on whenever they go outdoors. That is why so many of us drive alone, despite an abundance of high-occupancy lanes and admonitions to carpool. In general, when people say they would be afraid to pick up hitchhikers, the truth is that they simply don't want to stop, but think that fear is a more acceptable excuse than selfishness. And to those readers who recognize themselves in that last sentence, I would say: Don't worry. As someone who enjoys traveling solo, I completely sympathize. Drive on, wrapped in your private thoughts, and only stop when the urge moves you. If you don't pick me up, others will. Unless, of course, it's raining, in which case you should sacrifice your precious goddamn solitude and pull over.

Which almost wraps up this labyrinthine digression, but one last argument remains to be answered. Over and over, I have been told that hitchhiking was safer in the 1960s, or 1970s, but now the world is a more dangerous place. That is what the cop, for one, was telling me. And it is simply not true, either for hitchhiking or for life in general. This is not the place for a complex exploration of what has been dubbed America's "culture of fear," the perception of omnipresent dangers by people who in fact are as safe as they would have been fifty years ago. Television, movies, newspapers—but television overwhelmingly—have fed us such a diet of murders, rapes, kidnappings, and assorted mayhem from across the country and around the world that we tend to forget how little of this we know from personal experience.

In the case of hitchhiking, its most dangerous period was exactly the years that are now recalled as its heyday. In the sixties and seventies the highways were crowded with callow young travelers, and there were numerous stories of serial killers or rapists choosing their victims from the roadside smorgasbord. Not all of these stories were true, by any means, but some were, and they made a degree of sense: such was the array of vulnerable young people out on the roads, ready to climb into any car that stopped, that it is no surprise that they caught the eyes of potential predators. But that was when hitchhiking was in full flower, and so many of us were traveling on our thumbs that it was obvious that most arrived unharmed at our destinations. Today, the roadsides are empty and it is easy to conclude that this is due to new dangers. But the contrary is true. These days, not even the dumbest serial killer would be tempted to cruise the highways for young victims, because there are virtually none out there.

So yes, there are dangers involved in hitchhiking—just as there are dangers involved in riding motorcycles, in climbing mountains, in drinking whiskey—and I would not suggest that anyone should risk them if no commensurate pleasure is derived from the experience. But danger is not merely an awkward consort to adventure; it is what makes for adventure. From antiseptic office cubicles, escapists fly in droves to vacations as white-water canoeists or Arctic explorers. The dangers, statistically minimal but always hovering romantically around the venture like a covey of faintly menacing cherubim, are integral to the appeal. So why should I expend more space denying potential knights and adventuresses of the road the frisson of unknown perils? Let our half-stifled fears keep us awake as we roll down the interstate in the dry and cozy cab of a westbound semi.

CHICAGO INDEPENDENT

The cop was a talisman. Barely a minute after he had disappeared, a semi pulled abreast of my spot and the driver waved me over. As I approached, he leaned out the window, an old teamster's face under a rust-colored baseball cap, and asked me where I was headed.

"Towards Cleveland." I always say "towards," indicating direction, not "to," which might suggest that I want a ride to precisely that place.

"No, I'm not going that far."

"How far are you going?"

"I'm turning off at Springfield."

"Can you take me that far?"

He paused a moment, then nodded and gestured for me to climb in. I scrambled to get my pack, fold my umbrella, and run around to his passenger door. Speed is good manners, especially with truckers. I tossed my pack up onto the seat, grabbed the bar behind the door and swung into the cab, with my guitar in my spare hand, then fumbled everything into some sort of order as the truck got under way. The first ride always tastes sweet.

My driver looked to be in his mid-sixties, with salt-and-pepper hair at the edges of his cap and a white moustache. He had a slight accent, and turned out to be Polish, living in Chicago since 1961. The truck was his own. He had driven for various companies, then bought his first truck over ten years ago. Now he has three; his son drives one and they have one employee. His wife used to work as a secretary in a real estate office, but when he went independent she joined him to handle the orders. He called her on his cell phone, and they talked in Polish. His tone was affectionate, though when he translated the conversation to me it was all business. He was headed for Harrisburg, Pennsylvania, and she had found him a load to pick up there for Chicago. That is the goal of all trucking companies: always to be hauling something. It is difficult for small independents, but every mile you roll empty you are wasting time and fuel. So when you have a load going to Boston, you try to find another that you can pick up in that area and take somewhere else, then another there that is headed toward your home. This time it had all worked out, and if everything went smoothly he would be in his own bed by the next morning.

I checked my map and asked if he thought the rest area just before Springfield was a good one for me, or if there would be more trucks at the previous one. He said he had no idea, and we agreed that he would let me off at the last one. The more miles covered the better, especially with that cop on the road.

The driver passed me pictures of his family: A tattered, peeling, black-and-white snapshot from his wedding, his moustache black and pencil thin, his wife a broad-faced, smiling girl of nineteen, recently arrived from Poland. Then pictures of the children, four daughters and the son. All looked to be solid Slavic stock, big-boned and ruddy-cheeked, sitting around the kitchen table or posed in front of a meticulously ornamented Christmas tree.

"Do you ever go back to Poland?" I asked.

"I went back one time only, 1983. It is very sad there. No one wants to do anything. And the driving is terrible. People are being killed all the time. When I was in school there, I waited every morning at the bus stop and right there there were five people killed by cars, just while I was living there."

I asked if he still had family there, and he said yes, all of his family stayed except one sister who is in Chicago. I asked if things were better now that the Soviet Union was gone.

"No!" He was surprisingly vehement. "Before, it was better. There was order. The Communists, they kept everything in control. There was no crime, for example. Now, everyone is going crazy, the young people especially. It's not safe to walk on the street. It's like now in Iraq. Before, Saddam made a dictatorship and it was order, people could live their lives. Now, it's a mess. It's like a dog—excuse me, it's an example—it's just like if you have a dog, and you keep him chained up all the time in your yard, and then one day the chain breaks. He'll run like crazy, go all over and get lost, because he is not used to this. It is the same with people."

He told me that he mostly hauls produce: vegetables and fruit. He has been all over the country, but these days runs mostly between Chicago and the East—Boston, New Jersey, Pennsylvania,

Maryland, Ohio. "New England is good, very clean. Not so many blacks and Mexicans." He won't drive to New York City, because there are too many hijackings. "You have to know your way around. If you look confused, you get in a wrong neighborhood, some black guy will come up, very friendly, offer to show you the way, then he pulls out a gun and robs you. It's happened to so many drivers."

He made some business calls, flirting with the woman in the office of the vegetable warehouse in Harrisburg, checking in with the pickup his wife had arranged. There was some misunderstanding there, and he told them his wife would sort it out, then called her back to tell her what was going on. I had a moment's worry when he said he might have to leave the Turnpike at an earlier exit, but he got on the CB and found that the weigh station was open on that route, so we were back to plan A. He wasn't overweight—that is, the truck's load was within the legal range for its size—but he was behind on his paperwork, and filling out the forms plus queuing for the scales would waste too much time. I considered asking him to mention me on the CB and try to arrange a ride going west, but the sky seemed to be clearing and I felt like getting out and taking my chances. The rest area came into view, and he pulled in just long enough for me to jump to the ground, then rolled on toward the southbound turnoff.

MISSIONARY

I had been maybe five minutes in my new position—exactly like my first, perched at the juncture of the car and truck lots—when an extra-long pickup truck with a trailer behind it pulled over on my left. The driver was again a man in his sixties, but thin-cheeked and clean-shaven. He asked where I was headed, and if I could show him some identification. I gave him my driver's license and he looked it over carefully, then handed it back and asked me to open my jacket on either side so he could make sure I wasn't armed.

"I'm sorry, but I have to check you out."

"I understand. Of course. It makes sense to be careful."

"Careful." He fixed me with a serious look. "Not fearful."

Then he nodded and said he was going past Schenectady and I was welcome to come along.

When I was settled on the seat beside him, my pack next to me and my guitar between my legs, he continued: "Just so you know, I have a pistol, and my wife is in the car behind us, and she has a cell phone. So if you have anything in mind, we can take care of ourselves."

They were evangelical missionaries, working for a group that does Christian outreach to farmers. He had been a dairy farmer all his life, in southern Michigan, but five years ago had sold his farm to a nice young couple and retired. Since then, he and his wife spent most of the year on the road. In the summer and fall they traveled around to state and county fairs. In the winter, there were the big agricultural shows. Their only time off was a couple of months in the spring—planting season—which they liked to spend touring on his nine-hundred-pound Harley-Davidson. Motorcycles were his passion, and he kept wistfully pointing out groups of bikers coming toward us on the other side of the highway, returning from a big rally in Milwaukee. He had hoped to go, but there was too much work and he couldn't get away. His wife and he had spent the weekend setting up tents and training local helpers for three different fairs: in Connecticut, New Hampshire, and New York State, where they were headed now to break down the tent. Their ministry was all on a one-to-one or one-to-two basis, talking directly to individuals or couples, so at each fair they needed to have at least a dozen volunteers. They had spoken to over a thousand people that weekend, working sixteen hours a day and traveling between fairs in their time off.

He asked where I was from, and on learning I was from New England told a long story about how he and his senior citizens motorcycle club had gone up Mount Washington the previous year. He said he always tries to give people a lift when he can, and he isn't worried about having any trouble with them. "I have a .44 Magnum on my hip, and my wife carries a submachine gun." He glanced toward me, with a thin smile. "You can tell I like to joke around a little."

I told him about the woman who once picked me up in Montana and, with me sitting in the front passenger seat, warned me that I better not try anything because she had a gun in the glove compartment.

"And there you are, sitting right in front of the glove compartment." He shook his head. "What was she thinking of?"

He fell silent for a while, and I watched the scenery. There were patches of blue sky ahead, though we were still getting occasional sprinkles of rain. That stretch of the Berkshires isn't the most spectacular countryside, nothing that would look like much on a postcard, but there is something warm and inviting about the thick trees and unthreatening hills. It isn't wild, but it's country still, with plenty of space between the farms. Good hiking, good orchards, good dairies. At least, as a city boy, those were the images in my mind. The driver said the small farms were having a tough time. He was glad he got out of the dairy business when he did. He still wakes up at four o'clock every morning, though. There are some habits you can't break.

He was a calm man, not especially tall but holding himself straight in the seat, with short white hair, wearing a plaid lumberjack shirt, brown corduroy slacks, and work boots. He said that if I wanted to stop for an hour or two and help them with the tent, he could take me on to Syracuse, but otherwise he had to let me off at the second rest area after Schenectady. If he'd been offering a ride through to Michigan, I would have stuck around, but it was just another sixty miles so I said I'd just as soon keep going.

We had been riding about two hours, and I was relieved that my driver had not tried to bring me to Jesus. Especially in the United States, one gets to feeling a mix of gratitude and dread when drivers bring up the subject of religion. Gratitude because their beliefs prompted them to pick you up, and dread because the inevitable conversation is ahead. Once you have been asked if you know Jesus, the rest follows automatically, and much as I may respect a driver's faith and be grateful to be borne along as its fruit, the situation is uncomfortable and, especially at the dozenth iteration, mind-numbingly dull. I only once had a truly entertaining evangelist. He was French, and picked me up in Switzerland, in the rain. A picturesque fanatic, wild-eyed, bearded, and shaggy-haired, with hands alternately upraised to the heavens and desperately gripping the steering wheel, he told me how Christ had freed him from an addiction to heroin and could free me from sin. Not only that, but He would show me a miracle, right there and then: "Oh Lord, you who are all-powerful, show this young man what you can do! Stop the rain! Hear my prayer, Lord, you have done so much for me, now show yourself to this friend!" He moaned and yelled for half an hour, and eventually we hit a patch of clear sky. "You see?" He turned to me, triumphant. "Do you see the power of God? He heard my prayer and He has stopped the rain!" A few new drops splattered the windshield, but he was undaunted. "Do you see what faith can do?" The rain was falling faster, but he would not turn on the wipers and admit defeat. Finally, we were almost blind and he had no choice but to clear the windshield and go back to crying unto the heavens for a miracle. And so it went, for an hour and a half of intermittent showers, until I could stand it no more and asked to be let off.

So, as I say, I am genuinely grateful to all the people of faith who pick me up, but I was doubly grateful to this farmer-missionary for chatting about his work and his motorcycle trips rather than attempting my personal salvation.

Of course, I had relaxed too soon. We were passing Schenectady when he told me to pick up a little bracelet that was lying on the dashboard in front of me. It was a leather thong with six colored beads on it. "Do you know what those beads stand for?" he asked.

"No." But I could guess where we were headed.

"You look at that black bead. That represents the darkness of sin. We have all seen that darkness. I'm no different than you. I have sinned, and I have had that darkness in me. None of us are free of that.

"But you see that red bead? I know you've heard the story of Jesus Christ and how he died on the cross, but do you understand that he did that for you?"

I tried to make a noncommittal sound, indicating that I understood, but without sounding too enthusiastic; and I remained politely attentive. Some rides you pay for with polite attention.

"That red bead represents the blood of Christ, which can wash your sins away. And you see that white bead? Can you imagine what it feels like to be washed completely clean of sin? Can you imagine how it feels to know that whatever has happened in your life, whatever you have done wrong, He can lift that burden off you and make you pure and clean?"

His voice was soothing, and there was something sort of appealing in the idea of letting go, of giving up all doubt. Not a temptation to be converted right there on the highway, but a sense of what might draw someone to accept a higher power as responsible for their life, and let go of that weight.

"Now, look at that gold bead. That represents heaven. If this car was to veer off the road and we were both killed right this moment, do you know where you would go?"

"No, really I don't."

"Well, I know exactly where I would go. And because of that, I have no fear in this world. I may have good days and bad days, just like anybody else, but I know that they don't really matter, because this is all just a moment that will pass. Then my real life begins. That's a promise, a promise that God has made to all of us. We just have to accept Him and let Him into our hearts, and He will give us eternal life. Has anyone else ever offered you anything that precious?"

I never know what to say. I don't want to seem ungrateful, either for the ride or for the offer of everlasting salvation. I genuinely appreciated his taking the trouble to save me from eternal hellfire, as well as the gentle, polite manner in which he delivered his message.

He noted my hesitation. "I'm not trying to make you uncomfortable. But I care about you, and I want to do what I can to make your way easier."

"I appreciate that. And I don't mean to offend you . . ."

"You can't offend me." For the first time, he seemed irritated. "My faith is strong enough that you can't hurt or offend me. I have heard every argument or comment you might make, probably a hundred times over."

That was undoubtedly true. Neither of us had anything new to add on either side of the balance. But I was sorry for the strain in what had been a pleasant ride. Maybe he felt the same;

after riding in silence for ten or fifteen minutes, he made some innocuous comment about the foliage, and soon we were back to chatting about motorcycles. By the time he let me off at the service plaza, all was relaxed and friendly again. We wished each other well and he drove off, his wife giving me a smile and a wave from the car behind.

GODS OF THE HIGHWAY

There are drivers and there are hitchhikers, in life as on the road, in metaphor as well as in pickup trucks. My evangelist was a decent, intelligent man, but how could he not be struck by the ill-suitedness of his appeal: "If we crash right now, do you know where you are going?" How could I know if I was headed to heaven or hell, to the battlefields of Valhalla or the eternal boredom of Hades, or on a round-trip flight that would land me back on earth as a worm or a cocker spaniel? I didn't even know what state I'd sleep in that night, or where the next car might be headed. Drivers choose their destinations, follow their maps, plan the stops along the way. So fair enough, let a driver's religion promise a direct path to a predictable destination—always barring failures of faith or mechanics. A hitchhiker's religion has to be built on something else, or there's no sense in it. We make a blind leap into the hands of fate—or luck, God, angels, devils, what you will—assuming that we will be caught, and trusting that if we don't get where we planned to go, we may end up somewhere more interesting. I have often set out for one place and ended in another: The Monastery of Rondol in central France, where a driver took me because I was a musician and he thought I should hear the monks' Gregorian chanting, and where I spent three days. The monarch butterfly sanctuary outside Morelia, having been picked up by a naturalist guiding some rich tourists from Mexico City. A barium mine, two hundred meters down in a shaky, two-man elevator somewhere in southern Nuevo León, because a mining engineer had decided my life was incomplete without the experience. The French Alps, despite the fact that I was headed for Yugoslavia. Or simply the innumerable couches and spare beds in towns I had never heard of, far off any expected itinerary, where hospitable drivers chose to put me up, sometimes for one night, sometimes for days.

Hitchhiking is a gamble, and security is not what draws anyone to the side of the road. Which said, roadsides resemble casinos and foxholes as inspirations to situational piety. Living by chance, one cannot help seeing patterns in the way events fall out. You walk for hours in a Spanish desert, ignored by all traffic, then you reach an oasis, the adventure is over, and the first car that passes picks you up. A cop tries to run you off, you handle him appropriately, and he is barely out of sight before the long-awaited truck pulls over. After a while, you inevitably reach the conclusion that your choices affect your luck. If you are an optimist—and only an optimist will last any time as a hitchhiker—you cast this in terms of virtue rewarded. You are traveling with a friend and he decides he is tired of hitchhiking and will take a bus, while you insist on sticking out your thumb, and the result is that you arrive quickly and pleasantly, while your friend's bus is delayed, then breaks down, and he ends up having to hitch the same road in the dark, in the rain. It has happened to me, just that way. You trust the highway, and it takes care of you. Or, when optimism fails, you still judge your choices by the rides they bring. I was in Athens in August, faced with the decision of whether to go on through Greece despite the heat or to bail out and head north; choosing the latter course, but wondering if it was good sense or cowardice, I was picked up at the first tollbooth by a car headed for Lucerne, Switzerland—the gods were signaling that they approved my choice.

Hitchhiking is an exercise of faith, and the more you trust it, the more it rewards you. I have met many hitchhikers who refuse short rides, insisting that you go faster if you wait until a through-car stops. Some days, I'm sure they arrive ahead of me. Every day, though, they have longer waiting periods at dull entrance ramps, meet fewer people, and forego the potential rewards of chance.

Faith is a beautiful thing, if it gives you strength to do what you know you should be doing anyway. The more certain I am that if I take the less secure and more adventurous course the rides will arrive, the better my experiences on the road. It is not easy to keep that faith, and I freely concede that I have gotten a little rusty, a little too prone to stick to the well-traveled highways— but I count it a victory that after all these years I am out here at all. And what holds true on roads of tar and asphalt holds equally true on the metaphorical roads of our lives. How many of my friends, in various ways, decided it was more sensible to buy that bus ticket—signing on for a career that would carry them on a set route to a prescribed destination—and then saw their bus break down and found themselves one day out on the roadside, at a time and place they did not choose? If I have rarely known what I would be doing in a year, or where I would be living, something has always turned up. The trick is to keep your thumb out. The hitchhiker's philosophy is never going to be taught in high schools and colleges, designed to mold solid, dependable workers, but few of us have reliable bus lines in our lives. Whatever the road, there is always the chance of a breakdown, an unforeseen flat tire that leaves you unexpectedly stranded in the middle of nowhere. And if you don't know how to stick out your thumb and trust to the kindness of the drivers or the fates, then you're just damn well stuck.

But to return to the relatively prosaic roads we navigate in our cars: Hitchhiking can be a very fast way to travel, when the traffic is running your way, and all experienced thumbers take pride in knowing how to catch the right wave and surf straight and true to their chosen destinations. Myself, I have often boasted that I can beat Greyhound anywhere in the United States, and if anyone cares to put up the money I'll prove it tomorrow, rain or shine. But speed is not the reason any of us is out here, nor does any sensible hitchhiker make it a prime concern except on rare occasions. If you love the road, you are always ready to forget about making good time when tempted by a friendly driver or an intriguing side road, or a sign inviting you to visit the largest hand-dug well in the world—named, with typical Kansan understatement, "The Big Well"—where you learn that the Dalton Gang's hideout is just up the road. Pay a visit, and if you have good luck a fellow tourist will offer you a lift to this next site, and if you prove a pleasant companion he may turn out to be going another two hundred miles down the road into Texas.

Of course, maintaining faith is not always easy, especially when it is in little but a traveler's indefinite and transitory luck. I have been stuck on lonely stretches of road in the hot sun, without food or drink, and after a few hours have given traditional religion a shot, praying the stilted and most likely misdirected prayers of the tired and frustrated atheist in search of more substantial aid and figuring it can do no harm. Given enough hours at an abandoned crossroads, I have occasionally fallen to my knees like Robert Johnson in the song, and prayed to the good Lord to have mercy on me please—and eventually a car has always stopped, or I walked to a better place, or I curled up and slept there and got a ride in the morning. Were the gods just biding their time, or was it all sunstroke and desperation? In any case, dawn is an ideal time to hitch. Everyone who is up that early feels virtuous, and by being awake and traveling you automatically share that mantle of virtue. Sloth is handmaiden to all deeper sins, and the murderers and rapists are presumably sleeping in.

I have no reason to insist or evangelize, but my roadside mythology helps to keep me going. Hitchhikers are gamblers, and all of us have our lucky charms and pet superstitions. I don't carry a sign with my destination written in large letters, and I can give plenty of sensible-sounding explanations for that choice, but the real one is that when I hang out nothing but my naked thumb I feel more closely in tune with the universe. So there is my primitive and humble faith, and I settle for what fruit it provides. Wave the minister and his wife good-bye, and let's see which car stops next.

CHINESE-CANADIAN

TOURISTS

Speaking of the road-gods' rewards, the sun was out. I stripped the plastic bag off my guitar, folding it carefully and stowing it in my pack, then slung the instrument across my shoulder by its neck strap and started toward the exit ramp. A car was pulling out of the parking lot in front of me, and I waved a thumb in its direction. Simple as that, I had my ride. It was an Asian couple driving a car with Canadian plates, and they were headed for Buffalo. I climbed in the back, and we were off.

Both my hosts had strong accents, and after the initial exchange of greetings I asked where they were from.

"We are Canadian."

That wasn't what I meant, but on the other hand it was none of my business. "Are you on vacation?"

"Yes, we are one week in the U.S. We have seen Boston and now we are coming from New York. It is first time we visit."

"Did you enjoy New York?"

The woman shook her head violently.

"How about Boston?"

"Yes . . ." I had said I was from Boston, and she was trying to be diplomatic.

"Not so much, eh?"

Both of them laughed. She had a loud, happy laugh; his was more careful and polite.

He explained: They had grown up in Shanghai. "It was just the same as New York. Very big cities are all the same. Too many people, too big buildings. Too much hurry." They preferred Toronto. They came there from China ten years ago. They met in college in Shanghai.

"He played guitar in college," the woman told me, smiling. "That's why we pick you up."

The car had a CD player, and they were listening to John Denver's greatest hits.

"What kind of music do you play?" the man asked me.

"Folk, blues, different things."

"Do you like John Denver?"

"Sure."

The next song was "Country Roads," and he sang along. He knew all the words. Then he said something in Chinese, and the woman ejected the CD and replaced it with the Beatles' greatest hits.

He glanced back at me again. "Do you like Don Williams?"

"Yes, he's a very good singer."

"I like him very much."

Once again, the Don Williams phenomenon. When I was in Africa, it seemed as if everyone who saw me with a guitar, from Capetown to Kenya, immediately requested Don Williams songs. I eventually bought a bootleg cassette and learned a few of them, just to be polite. A lot of Americans prefer to think of jazz or rock as our great export, but in my experience country and western is the favorite American style around the world—and the smoothest singers are the most popular. Before Williams, it was Jim Reeves. Walking past a tiny village in central India, I was grabbed by a small boy who insisted that I must come meet his father, who loved American music. The father invited me into his house and showed me his record collection, a box of two dozen Jim Reeves albums. Ten years later, a man came up to me in a bar in Zimbabwe and said, "You are American? I love American music: Jim Reeves, Jimi Hendrix." Smooth, pretty singers rule the world. Learn Don Williams and Bob Marley, and you'll be popular anywhere on the planet.

My hosts watched the passing scenery and chatted in Chinese. It's relaxing to have a ride where you can sit in the back seat and not be the focus of attention. Another three hours to Buffalo, and with a little luck the next ride would take me through to Cleveland. My girlfriend had called some friends there, and they had said I was welcome to sleep on their couch. I'd never been to Cleveland; to me it was just a highway exit on the way to Chicago or Cincinnati. If the rides went right, I would be there by eight or nine, and if I got along with her friends and didn't seem to be overstaying my welcome I might spend a day checking the place out and visiting the Rock 'n' Roll Museum.

The Beatles album ended, and the woman flipped through a black leatherette folder of CDs and put on some Chinese pop music. It had female singers backed by lush, perky string sections and electronic keyboards. My hosts both sang along with all the songs.

I had been checking my map, and there was a service plaza just before Buffalo that looked as if it would be a good place for me to get out. By the time we got there it would be rush hour, but hopefully not too bad on the southeastern bypass, and there would be plenty of traffic headed toward Ohio. As we were coming up to Rochester, though, we passed a service area that was closed for repairs, and that got me a little worried. If the Buffalo one was closed as well, I would have no choice but to go into the city and spend the night there, and then I would have to find a way to get back on the highway in the morning—rarely a fun procedure. Or I could go to Canada, but Toronto was only an hour and a half from Buffalo, and would be no better when it came to hitching out again.

The next service plaza, west of Rochester, was packed, its regular traffic augmented by all the people who had wanted to stop at the closed one, and my hosts pulled in for a bathroom break. The gods had spoken. I thanked the Canadians and wished them a safe journey, then walked out to the confluence of the parking lots.

MEXICAN DRIVER

When the fish are biting, every hook will take. I hadn't even set down my pack before a pickup pulled over on my left. Or rather, two pickups, the first pulling a second that was tilted up with its front wheels on a two-wheeled tow dolly. I wasn't ready, and at first thought the driver was just pulling over to check something on the trucks, but he smiled and waved for me to come on. He had dark skin and a narrow black moustache, and up close his smile revealed a gleaming silver cap with a star cut-out.

"Where are you going?" The accent confirmed that he was Mexican.

"Cleveland."

"OK."

I got into the cab and switched to Spanish: "¿A donde va usted?"

"¿Hablas español? ¡Qué bien!"

He spoke hardly any English. He was trying to learn more, which was why he had picked me up, but since I spoke Spanish, we stuck with that. His name was Arturo, and he was headed for El Paso, then across the border to Ciudad Juárez. He was in a partnership with three other guys, buying cars and pickups over the Internet, then taking them down to sell in Mexico.

He explained that they did most of their buying in the Northeast; this time he was coming from someplace near Syracuse. He had driven up with a partner, who was headed south with a full load on their eighteen-wheeler car hauler while he drove the two pickups. Both of the pickups had been in accidents, but they still ran fine. They had cost fifteen hundred dollars each, and would sell in Mexico for twelve thousand dollars. Even adding in the travel and the import duties—NAFTA has done nothing for small businesses—it was a good profit. Arturo asked if I lived in Cleveland, and I explained that actually I was headed for Iowa, where I had friends, and had just picked Cleveland as a likely stopover.

"Then why not come with me to St. Louis? Isn't that closer to Iowa? I should be there around nine or ten tomorrow morning."

A tempting offer. I missed Mexico and was enjoying Arturo's company. And St. Louis was certainly a lot further along. I even had friends to stay with there. On the other had, I wanted to see Cleveland, and from there it would be a straight, easy shot along I-80 to Iowa City. On the third hand, my map did not suggest that getting out of Cleveland would be any kind of picnic: there is a spaghetti maze of downtown freeways, and highway planners give scant shrift to the needs of hitchhikers. It would be a full morning's work just to get back on the road. But on the fourth hand, what was the pleasure of hitchhiking if I let myself be trapped out on the freeway and couldn't stop where I wanted? I had time for a day or two in Cleveland, and what sort of lazy sod would pass up a visit just because it would take a bit of effort to get back to the highway?

Following this train of thought, I would soon have more hands than Shiva. And why make the decision now, in any case? We were not even in Pennsylvania yet, so Cleveland was more than two hours in the future.

The toll road ended at the Pennsylvania state line, and we were no longer limited to highway service areas if we got hungry. I hoped that, as a regular on this route, Arturo would be privy to a secret network of Mexican restaurants where even in the wilds of the Rust Belt one could get a decent bowl of chile verde. By now there are Mexican colonies in almost every part of the United States, and restaurants to feed them—or at least a convenience store or gas station with a sideline in fresh tamales—and it seemed simple logic that a Mexican truck driver would travel from oasis to oasis.

No such luck. Arturo was not aware of any oases east of Oklahoma, and in the meantime he was relying on Subway as the safest purveyor of gringo cuisine. He spotted one about half an hour into Pennsylvania, and I consoled myself by ordering extra jalapeños on my turkey deluxe.

It was nine o'clock when we reached the outskirts of Cleveland, and with Arturo heading south on 71, any place I got out would still be an hour from the downtown, even if there had been a decent place to get out—it was all highway, with nothing but forest and more highway as far as the eye could see. And it was dark, and might start raining again, and Arturo had taken advantage of my translation skills at the Subway and was pressing me to come with him to St. Louis. (Highway translation: another small service we hitchhikers provide. I once served as linguist and cultural go-between for a whole convoy of Moroccan immigrants on their way home from Germany—they actually offered to pay my bus fare back to France if I would stick with them until we reached the ferry at Gibraltar.) Arturo was quite capable of making his own way, but my presence made his life a little easier, especially if he had to drive through the night. So Cleveland remained nothing but a sequence of reflecting white letters on successive green exit signs, shortly followed by Akron, with Columbus ahead.

NIGHT

It was raining again, but now I found it soothing. I would be at least ten hours with this ride, and would cover more than five hundred miles, so current weather conditions were as immaterial as the gentle murmur of rain on a bedroom window when one is tucked warm under a down comforter.

I love gliding through the darkness, watching the broken white line flow under me like thread through a sewing machine, stitching me to the never-ending fabric of the highway. Rain just brings the darkness closer, turning the side windows into opaque sheets of black mica, reflecting the vague lights flashing past through the twin semicircles of cleared windshield. Road signs and tail lights, and the unfolding ribbon of gleaming asphalt. The slap of the wiper blades, the steady hiss of the heater, the undulating whir of wheels on wet pavement.

I was drowsing when Arturo pulled off at a truck stop outside Columbus. He was hearing a noise that bothered him, and as we slowed and made the turn it rose to a harsh, grinding clank. In the truck lot, we got out to survey the situation. It did not look pretty: The rear pickup was a little too wide for the dolly, so its left wheel did not fit completely within its assigned channel, and its deflated tire had slid over so that it was rubbing against the left wheel of the dolly. There was a canvas strap running around the front wheels of the pickup, and Arturo tried winching it tighter, so that it would pull the rubber folds of the empty tires away from the dolly's wheels. That looked a bit better, and worked long enough for us to get back on the highway, but in ten miles the noise was louder than ever. There was no option but to pull into another truck stop, run the metal ramps down from the back of the dolly and roll the rear pickup onto the ground, then try to remount it in a better position. This was a fairly involved project, since Arturo and his partner had removed the driveshaft of the towed pickup so that its back wheels would roll freely. I helped him lift the shaft out of the truck bed, then handed him wrenches as he lay on his back on the wet asphalt and wrestled it into place. Then he had to disconnect the tow lights and remove the wires running between the two trucks, switch the battery from the front truck to the rear one, get it started, and drive it back up the ramps so that it landed exactly where he wanted it on the dolly. Not an easy feat at the best of times, much less at night in the rain. To make it up onto the dolly, he had to back away and build up some speed, but because the dolly was so narrow he had to hit the ramps precisely to the inch, and all of this was being done on flat tires that folded and bunched and gave no traction. Plus, the front truck had to be kept immobile while the rear truck thumped into it from behind.

That was my job: to sit in the front truck and hold down the brake while Arturo galumphed up the ramps.

I was exhausted from the day's hitching, and wondering if we would ever get back on the road, or if I had made a wrong choice by skipping Cleveland and fate was punishing me by stranding me in the dark on a highway headed south, away from anywhere I wanted to go. Sitting in the front cab, jamming my foot down on the brake while Arturo backed off, then climbed my rump in a rumbling, shuddering assault, I felt as if I were trapped in the skull of a female elephant, stolidly bracing her for a clumsy, gargantuan coupling.

Arturo made four or five attempts before he was satisfied. This time, the right wheel overlapped instead of the left, but he lashed it securely and it looked possible, though far from elegant. Then he had to crawl back underneath and wrestle the driveshaft off again, rewire the lights, switch the battery forward, and slide the ramps back into the dolly. We drove out to the front parking lot, but by then it was obvious that things were even worse than before. Nothing for it but to quit or try the whole operation over again. And if we quit, then what? So we pulled the ramps down again, Arturo wriggled back onto the wet pavement with the driveshaft and his wrenches, I switched the batteries, and the elephants resumed their mating ritual.

It took another hour, but with much aligning and thumping and lashing we eventually got a couple of inches of clearance on either side of the tires and made it past Columbus without hearing any tell-tale whines or clanks. After all the tussling and frustration, though, Arturo was in no shape to drive four hundred more miles to St. Louis without sleep. We pulled into yet another truck stop, and he decamped to the rear truck, leaving me with the seat of the front cab. He even gave me his extra blanket.

The choice to leave me in front may not have been pure altruism. Some pickups have a flat bench seat, which makes a narrow but reasonably comfortable bed. The rear truck had one of those. In others, the bench is interrupted by a raised plastic section between the driver and passenger, which can be opened and used to store cassettes, paperwork, or what have you. This section is not raised very high, and might hardly be noticed by a casual observer. Even when I first lay down, with the storage compartment at my waist, it did not seem too bad. But it was just high and hard enough that any position I assumed would eventually begin to be mildly uncomfortable, then grow more so with every passing minute until I had to shift to another position. Nothing excruciating, but not conducive to a relaxed night's sleep.

At first, exhausted as I was, the discomfort hardly mattered. I arranged myself, lying on my side, with my face toward the windshield, Arturo's blanket over me and my jacket as a pillow, and dropped immediately off to sleep, lulled by the rise and fall of passing engines from the highway.

I woke an hour or so later with an ache in my side, turned over, fidgeted a little, and slept again. Then, as the night wore on, I tried more involved postures: curling into a tight ball on one half of the seat, with my legs sliding onto the floor and my head on the plastic mound, or piling my jacket alongside the mound as a sort of ramp down to the normal seat level. All in all, an exercise in wearied ingenuity, and never quite comfortable, but I slept more than not until a gray, wet light signaled the approach of dawn. With that first hint of day, I was wide awake, beset by the nervous impatience of the dependent traveler. Left to my own devices, I would have either gone into the truck stop and ordered a full-scale breakfast or hit the road, but the breakfast option was out, because Arturo had said he wanted to get an early start and I didn't want him to wake up and find me missing. Meanwhile, there was no sign of life in the rear pickup, and he certainly needed his rest.

With nothing else to do, I passed a long hour playing some quiet guitar and pacing the near side of the parking lot in the cold mist. This is when hitchhiking seems most illogical: I say I want to see the country close up, but it is a strange sort of tourism that leaves one acquainted with so many truck stops and service plazas and so few towns. Of course, this is not just a problem for hitchhikers. It is the curse and convenience of America's matchless interstate system. We can travel more miles in less time than in any other country, but the trade-off is that we see nothing but highway. In most parts of the world, you go more slowly, but you are constantly driving through towns and spend your nights in places where people live other lives. Here, as long as you are making a long-haul run, you live in a separate, long-haul world. It takes an effort of will to leave the interstates, and while that effort may be rewarded, the path of least resistance is to slip into the rhythm of the trucks and keep moving.

Arturo raised a drowsy head in the windshield behind me, and five minutes later emerged, rubbing his mussed hair and stretching his back in a creaky arc. "Let me just splash a little water on my face and let's get going. We'll eat and shower in a couple of hours."

TRUCK STOP

Yet another pleasure of hitchhiking: stopping for a shower. How many people crisscrossing the country in their cars have noticed the special privileges of the trucking fraternity? If they have remained oblivious, so much the better, because once aware of the apartheid of the highways, a car owner will forever feel a second-class citizen while on the road. Today's truck stop is not simply a restaurant and gas station that happens to have diesel fuel and an immense parking lot. It is a separate world, designed for truck drivers, and perceptive car owners are constantly confronted by signs reminding them that they are welcome up to a point, but must not presume anything like equality. There is a place for ordinary folk to eat, but the main dining area is labeled Drivers Only. And note the tone of condescension—it says "drivers," not "truckers," but all are assumed to understand the meaning: don't kid yourself just because you have steered a little metal box along a few hundred miles of highway. The real drivers are a separate caste.

The truck stop that Arturo selected for our morning break belonged to one of the main chains catering to over-the-road professionals, and its layout was typical: On the left, just past the entrance to the restaurant, there was a booth selling insurance, and next to it one hustling cell phones. In a large alcove to the right, after the double doors into the convenience store, was a bank of telephones and a half dozen screens for checking e-mail, as well as a RoadLink machine offering load matching, trip routing, permits, faxes, and copies. And between the store and the communications area, through a door marked Driver's Only, were the showers. Car owners, walk on by, this isn't your territory. For Arturo, though, it was a pleasure to be tasted in short order, and for me along with him—because there is an exception to the otherwise strict apartheid: study the No Hitchhiking sign stenciled on a truck stop's outer doors, and you will note that the prohibition applies to the action rather than its practitioners. Hitchhiking might be an annoyance to busy drivers, but hitchhikers, once they've become those drivers' guests, are honored alongside their gallant hosts.

So we stopped at a machine by the store entrance, where Arturo swiped his magnetic card through the groove and checked that he had enough fuel credits at this chain, then went to the booth in the middle of the store and got two keys, each tied to a wooden baton with a number on it. He handed one to me, and we went through the door to the shower hall.

Do ordinary motorists imagine the truckers hanging out back here like athletes gone to seed, a crowd of paunchy men in some big, sweaty locker room, working their T-shirts over their shoulders and stepping under a line of steaming shower heads? For all I know, there were truckers' showers like that sometime, somewhere—but not today in Ohio. We walked down an immaculate hallway, and were met by a polite attendant who directed us to our respective rooms. Spotless white tile set off a sink, a rack of fluffy white towels and washcloths, and a spacious tub. Once, showers might have been enough, but now the big chains vie with one another for clients who will maintain brand loyalty across the nation, and this is a luxury that counts. After ten hours' steady driving, the chance to lie back in a bubbly tank of hot water is an eagerly awaited and highly valued pleasure.

That may well be what Arturo did. Unfortunately, I had not asked him how long he planned to stop, and road etiquette required that I be ready whenever he emerged, so I had to settle for a shower. I didn't hurry it, though. I shaved, then stripped off my dusty clothes and turned round and round under the hot, massaging spray, rubbing away the road dirt and the uncomfortable night, and finally dried myself off with that rich towel—all the more enjoyable for being half-illicit luxuries.

Then I headed out to the restaurant, where of course I sat in the "drivers" area. A friendly waitress brought a thermos of coffee and a menu, took my order, and returned with a plate of fried pork chops, eggs over medium, hash browns, and wheat toast—the four basic food groups of a classic truck stop breakfast. I ate quickly, spurred by a combination of hunger and politesse, but when I had wiped up the last drop of egg with the last triangle of toast, Arturo still had not emerged.

Warm, clean, and full of food, I wandered across the lobby to the convenience store. There was a rack of postcards and one of candy for ordinary folk, but mostly the shelves were lined with a catalog of useful gizmos for the trucking trade: bunk warming pads—"Sleep warm without idling"—and sheets "specially designed to fit semi tractor beds." Ferocious alarm clocks with names like Screamin' Eagle, boasting, "Caution: Do not use near graveyards. May wake the dead!" Coolers, compact vacuum cleaners, coffeemakers, pizza ovens, fans, radar and laser detectors, power converters, and arrays of radios, CD players, televisions, and DVD decks. There was a section of CB gear, with six-foot-long antennas and speakers of all shapes and sizes. To one side of the cash registers, a locked glass case held pocketknives, hunting knives, and "hi-tech" knives with an array of specialized tools. Across from it was the music section—a bin of cut-rate cassettes giving way to racks of CDs. The selection was mostly country, along with rock and soul oldies, some heavy metal, and a couple of discs of rap. Over in the back of the store, a young woman stood behind a counter renting videos and books on tape, which could be returned at participating plazas down the road. The books included predictable trucker fare, from Louis L'Amour and Jake Logan's "Slocum" novels—"Today's longest running action western"—to Tom Clancy and Frederick Forsyth, but women have clearly become regular customers as well, and the warboilers sat side-by-side with Danielle Steele and Erica Jong. There was a stationery aisle, with log books, inspection reports, bills of lading, and Rand McNally StreetFinder and TripMaker software, across from a clothing section full of baseball hats, jeans, socks, underwear, and heavy-duty gloves. In a corner near the entrance, custom mudguards with silhouettes of buxom nudes hung beside a tastefully stocked rack of humorous bumper stickers. Lastly, across from the cash registers, a display of toy trucks ranged from matchbox miniatures to opulent radio-controlled Peterbilts, the perfect gift to remind children or grandchildren of their heroic roaming forebears.

I had been browsing through these offerings for ten or fifteen minutes when it occurred to me that I had gotten distracted, and Arturo might have made it out to the lot without my seeing him. Sure enough, when I went over to the pickups he was in the driver's seat, making himself a sardine sandwich. He offered me a can and some bread, and I apologized for keeping him waiting. No problem, he said, he had just gotten out there and needed a moment to eat. Another five minutes and, fed and refreshed, we were on our way to St. Louis.

MALAISE

Three hours later, the malaise set in. Maybe it was the sameness of the scenery, the intentional monotony of the interstates combined with the natural monotony of Midwestern topography. Maybe I was getting hungry again, or feeling the hangover from a bad night's sleep. Or maybe there was no particular reason. In every journey there are moments of doubt, and they often arrive without logic or warning. Thinking back on the years I have spent roaming romantic roadways in America, Europe, Asia, and Africa, I recall not only the adventures and friendships, but also the loneliness and the recurring questions: What am I doing here? Where am I going? Am I seeking my fortune or just running away—and if the latter, then from what? Responsibility, maturity, security, fears, weaknesses, strengths? I suppose at root the questions are universal. We are all on our various journeys and all beset by moments of doubt, indecisiveness, regret, or soul-deadening, dispiriting exhaustion. But as with so much else, the open road casts these moments in high relief, glaring and unavoidable. My father thought my love of hitchhiking was a sort of sickness, and he would be doubly sure if he could see me now. His motto when hitching was "Spend most of the time walking, cover most of the distance in rides." The walking, the chance to get out of the city and onto the quiet country roads was the point, and the hitchhiking a necessary evil. And here I am, midway through my forties, rolling down the narrow, gray channel of the interstate, bordered by concrete walls, highway signs, and billboards, passing towns unseen and stopping only at interchangeable, impersonal truck stops, eating a predictable, unhealthy meal, and rolling on. I can argue that I do this to meet interesting people, to cast myself upon the fates, to test my skills against chance and the elements, or just to sail with the raw, elusive winds of freedom, but I am in another battered pickup, driving down a flat, indistinguishable stretch of interstate somewhere in Indiana, or maybe it's Illinois, I can't even tell the difference since it all looks the same. Arturo is a nice enough guy, but so are they all, all nice enough guys, and maybe that cop was right and I am getting a little old for this. Not in the sense that I can't hack it, god forbid—I can still catch a night's sleep in the front seat of a pickup with the best of them—but in the sense of having better things to do. I expect to write about this, and I want to prove the naysayers wrong, to show that this is still an easy, friendly way to travel, and to urge a generation of young adventurers to try it on, but once I reach the West Coast and my point is made, maybe the time has come to call it quits. Do I really learn anything new by rummaging through the commercial detritus of one more fluorescent service plaza mini-mart? The interstates and chain stores have killed small-town America, and robbed the road of its haphazard, quirky soul. Sure, I could get off in Iowa and catch the smaller roads, but do I really want to spend an extra week that way, when I could barrel through to the Pacific and get this over with? But why be out here in the first place, if it feels like a chore rather than a free-wheeling flight above the prairies? In any case, there's no point turning back at this stage of the journey, and even if there were, how would I turn back? Get a cramped, uncomfortable seat in a Greyhound bus, traveling more slowly down the same highway and exchanging plastic truck stops for run-down urban bus stations? And how would I explain a decision to bail out before I even crossed the Mississippi, less than two days from home? Obviously I'll push on, even if all I'm doing is sacrificing a week to nostalgia and stupid pride. An old lesson, ever learned anew: the hitchhiker's most constant, implacable enemy is not harsh climates or demented drivers, but simple boredom.

ROUNDING ST. LOUIS

rturo let me off at the last rest area before St. Louis. We had been almost twenty-four hours together, but we parted with no exchange of addresses, phone numbers, or even last names. Just the formulaic hope that we would meet each other again, someday, somewhere down the road.

It was three o'clock. I had called my friends in St. Louis, but they were out of town. I could have gone in anyway, but once again the simpler course was to go around and keep rolling. With good luck, I could still make Iowa City that evening. Even if I didn't, I would be off the interstate, tracing the Mississippi River north on Highway 61, and I would find someplace to sleep along the way. First, though, I needed a ride that would take me past the city.

Here was a moment for strategy and technique. If I just stood at the highway entrance ramp, I would be wasting precious time and effort. Most drivers would assume that I either needed a ride into the city or wanted a long-haul lift. The St. Louis rides would be of no use to me, while the long-hauls would be split between those who thought I was headed down I-44 toward Oklahoma and those who thought I wanted I-70 to Denver. In fact, I wanted to go a mere sixty miles on 70, then head north, but no one would guess that, nor could I convey it easily with a sign. The time had come for the direct approach. I was at a basic rest stop: no restaurant or fuel, just toilets and telephones. A perfect situation, because everyone who pulled in would be making only a brief visit, and going up the same path to the doors. I did notice that the posted list of rest area regulations prohibited hitchhiking, but there seemed little point in dwelling on this detail. Better to focus on the task at hand.

The weather was sunny and warm, so I seated myself on the low stone wall outside the doors and played a gentle tune on my guitar. A trucker walked by, headed inside, and I begged his pardon and said I needed a ride out 70 to 61.

"No, I'm headed down 44." He walked a few steps further, then turned. "If I was going that way, I'd help you out." A good sign.

A man came out of the building, and I made the same pitch. Not pushy, just sitting comfortably in the sun, playing some music, happy to be where I was, but ready to travel when someone happened to be going the right way. And he was. "Sure, come on. I'll just need a minute to clear off the other seat."

He was an old-time over-the-road semi driver, with Merle Haggard on the tape deck and the CB keeping up its constant, staticky crackle. Gruff, laconic, a lone ranger and not looking for company, but sympathetic to the problem of getting through the urban morass, and willing to lend a hand.

Even at three thirty, on the outer ring road, the traffic was getting thick, and my driver's mood congealed along with it. "It gets worse every year. An hour from now, this'll look like a fuckin' parking lot." To your classic trucker, cars are irritating vermin, cluttering the road and prone to unexpected and dangerous whims. Back in the days of the CB craze, when Rosalyn Carter set a national model by signing on as "First Mama" and truckers were portrayed as movie and television heroes, they saw their admirers as a chattering infestation of uppity mice. I particularly remember one who picked me up outside Detroit, his eyes glinting with amphetamines after thirty uninterrupted hours on I-80: At the top of every hill, he would scan the traffic ahead until he spotted a car with a CB antenna, then bear down on it at top speed, laughing over the airwaves like a demonic avenger: "Breaker, breaker! You down there in the blue Chevy. You better get the hell out of the way, because I'm coming through!" It was not the most relaxing ride, especially since he was carrying a load of hanging beef, which he cheerfully explained was more dangerous than dynamite because if he hit a curve too fast it would swing and pull the whole rig over on top of us. Still, as Mark Twain said of steamboat crashes, it would make good literature.

My current driver, slowed by the afternoon sludge, limited himself to contemptuous grumbling: "See that guy down there? Look at him, he's working on a laptop while he drives. You see that all the time: people eating lunch, doing paperwork. Reading books! You see 'em out there doing seventy, with a book on the steering wheel. There's this one woman works with my wife, she tells me she can do her paperwork and change into her business clothes while she's driving in to the office. People are fuckin' crazy. Why doesn't she just pull over at a rest stop. It would probably end up being quicker. And then they wonder why there are so many accidents . . ."

Amateurs do dumb things, and professionals end up in accidents, and then politicians make some new laws and insurance companies hike their premiums, and it gets harder and harder to feel like the last American cowboy when you are fenced in by regulations and tracked by satellite. My driver's new pet hate was satellite positioning devices. Nowadays, someone sitting in an office can click on a screen and see your exact whereabouts, check your speed, then call you in your cab and bitch at you. He doesn't have that problem yet, because he drives for an owner-operator with just a half-dozen rigs, but he hears about it from the other drivers. "I don't know anybody who likes the damn things. Of course, guys have figured out ways to mess with them. They get inside the box and turn 'em off, and if the boss asks they just say there must have been some kind of interference. They keep making rules, but people will always find a way to get around 'em."

There was no place to pull over at the Route 61 exit, but the traffic had thinned a little and my driver just stopped in the right-hand lane. I jumped out and headed for the ramp.

WEIRDO

I didn't even make it halfway down the ramp before a car pulled over. The driver was only going twelve miles, to someplace called Moscow Mills, but anyplace would be better than where I was. There was construction going on around the intersection and no place a sensible driver could have stopped.

I was grateful, but also glad that it was a short ride. My new host was a young guy, paunchy, scruffy, unshaven, and bare-chested, wearing only a pair of khaki shorts. He was steering with his left hand, and his right was in his lap, rubbing his crotch. I kept my pack in front of me and my guitar propped between my legs, to allow for a rapid exit and discourage any potential advances.

He drove a little way in silence, then glanced over at me: "Aren't you awful warm in that shirt?"

"Nah, I'm fine, thanks."

He turned the radio up. It was tuned to a classic rock station, with more ads than music. He didn't say anything more, just watched the road and massaged his shorts, and occasionally looked over at me, then quickly back at the road. We passed Moscow Mills, and then he said, "My place is just two blocks from here, on the right, so I'll let you off at the gas station." He pulled over and I got out. Another twelve miles covered.

REGIONAL MANAGER

I was off the interstate, on the mythic Highway 61, but it was still a four-lane, divided road. A police car had pulled over a speeder a hundred yards before the gas station where I was standing. I was pretty sure that it was legal to hitch on state roads in Missouri, but there was no point in pushing my luck, so I went into the station and bought a bottle of orange juice, then hung out by the pumps, drinking it, until the cop finished his business, made a U-turn, and disappeared toward the south. Then I walked out to the corner, propped my pack against a sign, and started hitching. It was the first time this trip that I had been able to stand out on the roadside rather than at a rest stop or service plaza. It felt good, though the traffic was annoyingly local. Drivers kept signaling that they were turning off shortly, or just running errands, or that they would not be leaving town. Familiar gestures: the first, a finger pointing right or left; the second, a finger pointing down and revolved, as if stirring something; the third, a finger pointing at the dashboard, bobbing up and down. Where do drivers learn those signals? I have seen them all over the world, but only when hitching, so where do the non-hitchhikers pick them up? Maybe they are hard-wired in the brain. In any case, I find them encouraging; when a lot of drivers take the trouble to signal that they can't carry me, that suggests that they are aware of my existence and feel a need to explain why they aren't stopping. I always smile and nod, to show that I understand. It's like the panhandlers who say "God bless you, have a nice day" when you mumble that you have no spare change. Be polite today; you may be rewarded tomorrow.

I was there for fifteen minutes, my longest wait since Boston. I was hoping for a ride up to Iowa City, but I didn't expect to find a through car right away, and I wasn't sweating it. The sky was clear, and I was glad to be on something more like a normal road. If I didn't make it tonight, I'd make it in the morning, and if I didn't find someone to put me up, I could sleep rough for one night.

A bearded guy in a battered red pickup sort of half pulled over, gesturing up the road. I didn't know what he was getting at, so started toward him, and he rolled down his window and yelled, "There's your ride!" I looked around, and sure enough, there was a big white Ford backing up in the breakdown lane.

The Ford stopped when I started running toward it, and the door opened on the passenger side. When I reached it, the driver was on the phone, so I climbed in quietly and he pulled back onto the road. He was a big man, probably in his mid-forties, with a dark moustache. He had a suit jacket laid out on the back seat and was in a light blue button-down shirt, with a couple of pens in the pocket. He was talking on a cell phone, explaining to someone about a printing job they had to get ready before five. He repeated his instructions twice, sounding patient but rolling his eyes at me to indicate the slowness of his interlocutor.

After five or ten minutes, he signed off, apologized to me, but explained that he had to make a couple more calls because we would soon be in a dead area where his phone didn't work. They were all business calls, coaxing a new employee through the process of negotiation with an irritated manager, congratulating a salesman who had just signed up a big order—"That one, he's quite a story," he told me between calls. "He's from Oklahoma, dresses like a cowboy, and he has multiple sclerosis, he's having trouble walking, and he's the best salesman I've got. Little, skinny guy, but he can sell like nobody's business." Then he was telling someone else to "set up the table however looks good to you" and he'd check it all when he got there. "She's new, and she doesn't know a damn thing about power tools, but she's a real eager beaver. She came in for the job interview with her husband, and he said he'd help her out, so I decided to give her a break and I think she's gonna work out fine. I just wish she had a little more self-confidence—she keeps calling me about every little thing comes up."

He was the regional manager for an international power-tool manufacturer, some name made up only of initials, which he explained was the parent company, making tools that got sold by a variety of suppliers under other brand names. They had an exclusive contract with Home Depot, and he was on his way to Quincy, Illinois, where a new superstore opened a year ago. They'd been having some problems, sales were lower than projected, so they had called in all their major suppliers for an in-house trade show and conference. He manages the whole region, all of Missouri down into Arkansas and southern Illinois—a lot of driving. "I always pick people up. Always have. We had a discussion in my church three weeks ago, talking about how you should help out other people as though they were Jesus Christ, and somebody brought up hitchhikers, and don't you know ninety-five percent said they wouldn't stop for anybody? But what if it was Jesus and he was testing you? They said you have to be careful these days, but I don't worry about it. I was a fullback all through high school and college. I'm not as fast as I used to be, but I still have plenty of firepower."

He grew up in a small town in southern Missouri, and he's sorry to see that way of life disappear. "It was your typical small town, with a main square and all the businesses on one street, but you know we used to have three grocery stores, all three of them little places with just one aisle in the center. I really miss that, it was a good place to grow up. I often think that if I won the lottery I'd like to go back there and put some of that stuff back. Of course, it couldn't support three grocery stores, but it would be nice to have one."

He asked me how far it was to Quincy, since I had a map and he didn't. It was about forty miles. He was planning to cross the river at Hannibal. I hinted that he might go on another twenty-five miles to Taylor and cross there, but he said he was kind of in a hurry and they'd told him this was the fastest way. Frankly, it looked like the fastest way to me, too, but I'd figured I had nothing to lose by hinting. He asked me if I could find Ashton on the map; he knew it was somewhere above Hannibal and he had to go up there in a couple of weeks because his youngest son had a football game. He had three sons, and they all played.

I planned to get out when he left 61, and to try to make it through to Iowa City. It was about five thirty by now, so I still had a couple of hours of light, and since most of the long-distance traffic would probably be headed that way, all I had to do was catch a ride through before dark. But then, coming up on Hannibal, we began passing signs for Mark Twain sites and the "historic waterfront," and suddenly things looked very different. I was in no hurry, and why take a chance on getting stuck out on some godforsaken stretch of road when the path of righteousness so obviously led to stopping and paying homage to Huckleberry Finn? "What the hell, I'll turn off with you and go to Hannibal." My driver thought that was pretty funny, but he had no objections, and five minutes later he dropped me at the off-ramp for the historic district.

THE LITERARY LIFE

We all have debts to pay, even if only in our minds. Mark Twain may be nothing more than a great writer to some people, an entertainer and erstwhile philosopher long dead and hallowed in the musty academic canon, but I owe him my life. Twain, Woody Guthrie, Robert Louis Stevenson, Lloyd Alexander—I believed every word they wrote, and as soon as I was old enough I set out into the world, using their writings as my Baedeker and Michelin.

I thought of Tom and Huck as friends and companions, and trusted to the truth of their adventures—of course Twain invented the stories, but there is a world of difference between fact and truth—and I wanted to have my own. When I was told that times had changed and it no longer made sense to just throw a bundle over my shoulder and go off to seek my fortune, I always asked,

"Why not?" In almost thirty years, no one has come up with a persuasive answer.

There was no golden age of romantic wanderers, and I am not out here pursuing a vanished way of life. The road always had dangers, and never promised anything but occasional adventure and frequent discomfort. I regret the invention of passports, but do not regret missing the chance to be burned as a witch, tossed in jail for vagrancy, or impressed into the king's navy. For as long as I've been traveling, people have been suggesting that I belong in another time—some imagine me as a medieval minstrel, others on Twain's Mississippi River or hoboing along with Jack London or Jack Kerouac. But those are the fantasies of the imaginers, who believe that they are trapped by the prosaic present and that in more romantic times they too would have been out on the road. For myself, I've never regretted that I'm living in the here and now. The world is constantly changing, and when the traveling gets easier in one region, it gets harder in another. Other times offered other pleasures, but this one is as good as any.

As to basing a life on novels and legends, what better guide could there be? A writer you enjoy is a friend, and a friend's description of a place, a person, or an experience is always more valuable than dry, supposedly impartial reportage. Even if that friend's description is invented or imaginary, it is always based on something, and at least with my choice of writers, it is not trammeled by too much caution. The guidebooks consistently err on the side of caution, especially in these litigious times when someone might haul a publisher into court for leading them into danger. Not one of the many tourist guides to the Andalusian mountain town of Ronda mentions the rusty staples nailed at odd intervals into the rocks above the river, by which one can clamber up the cliff face, emerging in the backyard of an annoyed householder—and yet, that is obviously the path Tom Sawyer would have recommended to get from the riverbed to the town.

As any reader will remember, Tom himself took storybooks as his models. One could argue that he ended up in some unnecessary scrapes as a result, and sometimes led his friends astray, but I would counter that it is exactly those scrapes and straying that gave his life its savor and make the books fun to read. He is often wrong, but never dull, and while success has indisputable advantages, so do romance and picturesque experiments. Of course, you can read Tom's story and conclude that he is welcome to his adventures but you would rather stick to the straighter, less flamboyant path of his half-brother, Sid. You certainly will have no lack of company. The world is full of Sids, and they manage everything and keep it all functioning. And considering how well it functions, on their heads be it.

Along with inspiring me to get out on my own river and see the wide world, Twain also provided a wealth of entertainment on the journey. His travel writings, though rarely read today, have been for me a recurring pleasure. Recently, rereading *Life on the Mississippi*, I even found a passage that opened up my own world to me, and made me understand just what I have gained from hitchhiking. He was describing his years as an apprentice pilot, and the range of people he served under while pursuing that profession:

> I am to this day profiting somewhat by that experience; for in that brief, sharp schooling, I got personally and familiarly acquainted with about all the different types of human nature that are to be found in fiction, biography,

or history. The fact is daily borne in upon me, that the average shore-employment requires as much as forty years to equip a man with this sort of an education. When I say I am still profiting by this thing, I do not mean that it has constituted me a judge of men—no, it has not done that; for judges of men are born, not made. My profit is various in kind and degree; but the feature of it which I value most is the zest which that early experience has given to my later reading. When I find a well-drawn character in fiction or biography, I generally take a warm personal interest in him, for the reason that I have known him before—met him on the river.

Hitchhiking serves one similarly, as a sort of commonplace book of humanity, a volume of scraps and vignettes which I unconsciously consult as I read, talk, or watch a movie, and by which I judge the truth of what I am reading, hearing, or seeing. There are conversations that ring true, resembling as they do the monologues of some forgotten driver, and others that immediately strike me as false, since they do not sound like anything said by any of that vast and varied multitude. Admittedly, my commonplace book is a bit different from Twain's. He dealt not only with decent captains who taught him the trade, but also with brutal ones who acted as if he were a nuisance and intruder in the pilot house. By contrast, I meet only the people who stop to give me a lift. They are a bizarrely assorted bunch, including some decidedly unlikely Samaritans—there was a fellow who picked me up in North Dakota and took me all the way across Montana, but sent me into restaurants to get food for him because he was a raving paranoid and sure that the other customers were robbers or right-wing vigilantes. Still, all of those drivers were hospitable enough to give me a lift, and my generally sunny view of humanity may be largely traceable to the fact that I never met the people who passed me by.

At least in his later years, Twain's view was far darker. He had seen too much misery and failure to preserve the Sawyerian optimism of his youth. As a reader, I appreciate his cynicism and bitter humor, and will not deny the wisdom in it. But the lessons of Twain's old age, though bleaker than the lessons of his youth, are no more profound. Every stage of life has its wisdom, and all of us write the book of our own experiences and draw the lessons we will, or can. Twain reached an age where he looked back and saw youthful hopes dashed and little to be truly valued in life. I have not reached that point. Does that prove my lack of wisdom? If so, it is not a sort of wisdom I am in any hurry to attain.

In any case, further introspection can wait for a day when I am stuck out on a boring entrance ramp without a ride. For now, Hannibal is waiting.

HANNIBAL

Sometimes everything just feels right. As I walked down the hill toward the old town center, every step sent a spray of crickets leaping through the grass ahead of me. I had climbed off the roller coaster, and the evening was spread out before me, slow and deep as the Mississippi itself. Sleeping would be no problem: The road was lined with pine forest, offering plenty of sweet-smelling shelter and privacy. Or, if the town proved friendly, there might be a bed somewhere. Either way, it was a good place to be Huckleberry Finn.

There were signs everywhere for Twain sites: his birthplace, Becky Thatcher's House, Injun Joe's Cave. And other signs: A block above the downtown, a stark billboard proclaimed in black on white, "Pray that George W. Bush does not forget God's covenant with Israel," and cited Genesis 15:18, about the land being given forever unto the seed of Abraham. It was a treat to imagine Twain's response to that one.

Turning onto Main Street, the Twain museum and his boyhood home were on my right. There was a small garden separating them, with a patch of trees at the back—another possible sleeping place. Around the corner was a little, cobbled street, the heart of historic Hannibal. It was lined with period houses, each labeled to show its place in Twain's life. Across from his boyhood home was "Becky Thatcher's house"—wrong, as any Tom Sawyer reader knows—and next to it, the newspaper and law offices where Twain's father worked and where the young Mark (or rather, Samuel Clemens) served a brief apprenticeship. All very nice, in its way, but I was headed for the river.

I grew up by the ocean, with a love of deep water, waves, wind, and distant lands imagined somewhere out beyond the islands and the horizon. And yet, I read Twain early and like all his youthful acolytes I got the Mississippi in my blood, thick with Ohio mud, ghosts, and fantastic adventures. The historic preservation office can turn old houses into museum exhibits, but it can't embalm the river. When Hannibal and Twain are both forgotten and the only things walking are cockroaches, the Mississippi will still be flowing thick and careless as ever.

Down across the railroad tracks, past a small square harbor of bobbing motorboats, to where a little side-wheeler steamboat stretched out alongside a grass-grown, rocky pier. A placard announced that the dinner cruise would start in fifteen minutes, a two-mile journey complete with steam calliope music and a Mark Twain impersonator. Huck or Tom would not have given it a second glance.

I walked along the pier, to where it made an elbow shielding the harbor, then clambered down from the crumbling cement path to seat myself on a rock where I could listen to the gently lapping water. On my left, the bridge to Illinois arched against the dimming sky, cars and trucks passing in a rumble that carried clearly over the water. A coal barge, long as a football field, floated past like a sleeping giant, bound downriver to St. Louis and maybe on to New Orleans. If you caught it at a lock, you might be able to hitchhike it. If you were Huck, you might swim out and stow away. Summer thoughts, to be filed away for another visit.

I played a light tune, in time with the water. Two teenage girls, slim and blonde, escaping a family picnic in the park on shore, walked past to the end of the pier and snuck a cigarette. The dinner cruise pulled out and headed upriver, a loudspeaker announcing the historic menu ahead. I was looking for Huck's island, but the water stretched uninterrupted to the Illinois bank. Maybe it was right in front of me and the distance made it seem a part of the far shore, or maybe it had long since fallen prey to erosion or the Army Corps of Engineers. Or maybe Twain made it up, remembering another island and moving it over to this patch of river, where it would come in handy for runaways.

The shadows had disappeared and the air was getting cool. I shouldered my pack and climbed back to the walkway. Time to see what Hannibal had to offer. Except that fate had a final present in store, capping the romantic hobo reverie: as I approached the tracks, bells began to ring, the gates came down, and a freight train hove around the bend from the south. I leaned against a wooden telephone pole, pulled my guitar into position, and stood there picking train songs. The clatter of the wheels drowned the music, but I could feel the melodies in my fingers. It was a long train, and took two and a half songs to pass. All flat-sided grain cars—the only way to ride them would be to climb up the ladder and sit on the roof. Still, to anybody raised on Twain and Woody Guthrie, every train is a temptation.

HOPPING FREIGHTS

Why are there so many train songs, and so few about hitchhiking? Even those few are mostly 1960s rock and soul tunes, unsuitable for singing as one walks down a country road: Marvin Gaye's "Hitch Hike," Vanity Fair's "Hitchin' a Ride," Jimi Hendrix's "Highway Child." Not bad songs, and of course there's "Me and Bobbie McGhee," but put those up against all the songs about riding freights. I once sat in a freight yard outside Spokane and tried to run through all the train songs I knew: "Hobo's Lullaby," "Waiting for a Train," "Jay Gould's Daughter," "Wabash Cannonball," "Starlight on the Rails," "East Texas Red," "Hard Travelin'." I guess I was pushing it a little when I got to Guthrie's "Vigilante Man," but I had just heard about a gang of vigilantes who had shot a hobo outside the yards in Wishram.

So there I was, singing, "What is a vigilante man, tell me what is a vigilante man? Does he carry a gun and pistol in his hand . . ." when suddenly an electronic speaker mounted on a pole a few feet away from me crackled to life and a voice boomed forth: "If you really want to know, Dylan, we got a couple here we could send out to you!"

That was during my brief experiment in train-hopping, a journey from Davis, California, up to Portland, Oregon, and then across to Minneapolis. It was pretty easy. I just left my pack and guitar with a friend, walked into the dispatcher's office in Davis, and asked when a freight was due to come through heading north. "I hope you're not thinking about riding any freights," the dispatcher said, in a fatherly sort of way. He was in his fifties, with wire-rimmed glasses. "A lot of people have gotten hurt that way, fallen off and lost an arm or a leg. Plus it's against the law. So when that Portland train comes through at eleven fifteen, I don't want to see you anywhere around here. And I hope you're not going to be like those guys who wait in the trees around the curve down there, and climb on while the train stops for ten minutes." I thanked him, and said of course not.

There were no open boxcars, and the gondolas I looked into were full of black, nasty-looking grime and twisted bits of loose metal, so I ended up on a piggyback, a flatcar with two truck trailers on it. Hoboes will tell you not to ride piggybacks, because if there is any kind of accident you can easily end up crushed under a semi trailer. An experienced hobo might have gone off and bought a bottle, got some sleep, and caught out tomorrow. Or, like me, he might have said "Fuck it," and climbed onto a piggyback. If the damn things crashed all that often, the freight companies wouldn't use them.

It wasn't the most comfortable night I'd ever spent, but it wasn't supposed to be. I got some sleep and watched a lot of dark lumps of trees slide past, and saw all the stars you never see in town. Somewhere, up at the front of the train, there must have been a few lights, but I sure couldn't see them—there are lots of forms of transportation that are faster than freight trains, plenty that are more comfortable, and very few that aren't cleaner, but for sheer length they are in a class by themselves. Sitting on a car in the middle of a train, you rarely see either end. Nor is there much chance that any of the trainmen will see you. We stopped only once that night, and after a while I heard the crunch of boots on gravel and saw a flashlight beam a dozen cars up, but whoever it was never got back to me, and after another half hour we clanked on toward Oregon. The sunrise woke me as we rounded Mount Shasta, and anyone who would not have fallen in love with the freights at a moment like that should just get a job in a bank and be damned.

I spent the next morning wandering Portland's skid row, then caught an eastbound train late in the afternoon. The Pacific Northwest is a sort of haven for hoboes, with lines of missions where you can get a free meal if you don't mind listening to a prayer, or a bed when the weather gets nasty. A lot of guys prefer to sleep out, whatever the weather, because nobody checks your breath for alcohol, and a bedroll under a bridge with your buddies and a bottle can be warmer than all the cots and blankets in all the missions on earth.

The general run of longtime hoboes take pride in looking after one another, and on the yards in Portland I was befriended by a middle-aged black guy named Joe, who found us a flatcar headed for Spokane. We settled ourselves at the front of the car, where a four-foot-high metal lip would break the wind, and just as we were pulling out three more hoboes came alongside, two big, burly, red-bearded men carrying an old guy who could hardly walk. They rolled him onto the car, then jumped up after him.

The new arrivals settled down at our feet, and the bigger of the bearded men pulled a little plastic-wrapped packet of cheese and crackers out of his shirt pocket and tried to get the old man to eat. "You have to get something in your stomach. You can't just live on liquor." Joe looked at me and shook his head. The old man was clearly not going to be around much longer. I was struck, though, by the tenderness with which his companions treated him. He was weak, dirty, and drinking himself to death, but I couldn't see where he would be better off dying in bed in a VA hospital rather than out here with his buddies.

They were headed to Pasco, Washington, at least for the time being. There was a sort of flophouse or mission there—I never sorted out exactly what kind of place it was, but apparently it was run by a woman who would give the old man a bed and get some food into him. They asked where we were headed. Joe said he was going to Spokane. I said I was planning to try to get all the way to Boston. They looked a little puzzled by that. "Do you have a driver's license?" the big guy asked. I said yes, and he asked, "Then why don't you go down to the welfare office and get a check, and buy a bus ticket?"

I said I wanted to try riding the trains, and gestured at the view. It was worth gesturing at. We were following the Columbia gorge east, with the river spread out on our right between high, orange-white banks, and the sun setting behind us. The other guys agreed that it was a pretty sight, but they still thought Boston was a long way to travel on the freights.

The big guy and Joe got to talking. The old man had his eyes closed, with his head cradled in the smaller guy's lap. The smaller guy hardly spoke, but listened to the conversation and nodded along with whatever his partner said. To me, there was something unreal about it all, as if I were watching a movie about old-time hoboes. They talked about bumming to "Frisco" and "Chi," about their days in the service and how their marriages went to shit. Then the conversation turned to detoxification wards around the country. "Don't ever let yourself get put in detox in Salt Lake City," Joe warned. "It's the worst I've ever seen, just cots and plain white walls. They don't even have a television."

Most places were better than that, apparently, and my companions were equipped to discuss their relative merits in some detail. It was not a conversation I would have imagined hearing in this or any other setting, and it provided an excellent corrective to the romance of the scenery and the communal feel of our little company. It also provided me with my favorite hobo quotation of all time, spoken with great emphasis by the big guy: "Man, Tacoma is the Cadillac of the detoxes!" Should anyone in the Tacoma mayor's office be reading this, I offer that one free of charge as a new city motto.

It got dark and chilly, and the old man began to shiver and mumble, then to moan quietly. We all chipped in our jackets to cover him, but the cold wasn't really the problem. He needed a drink. The next freight yards were in Wishram, but Joe warned the others not to try them. A hobo had been shot there the previous week, and word was out that it was no random incident, that the shooter was one of a group of local citizens who were sick of all the bums wandering around town and had organized a vigilante committee. The big guy had heard the same rumors, but he also knew a bartender there who accepted food stamps for booze, and in any case the old man couldn't stay on that flatcar. Between the shakes and the cold and the constant bounce and sway, he was hurting bad. So when the train slowed down in the Wishram yards, the big guy jumped off and ran alongside, and his partner rolled the old man off into his arms, then jumped and joined them. "Stupid," Joe said, as they disappeared in the darkness. "That old man shouldn't be on the trains at all, at his age. Some people just don't think."

The whole experience reminded me of some lost episode from Woody Guthrie's *Bound for Glory*—which is why I had hopped a train in the first place. We didn't sing together, but if it had been daylight and a longer run, it wouldn't have surprised me if one of the other guys had borrowed my guitar and sung some Hank Williams, and I might have done one of Woody's train songs and they would have nodded along with the lyrics. It was a sociable scene, a little society of like-minded souls. Which I suppose is why there is a hobo culture and no hitchhiking culture. Hoboes ride and camp together, sharing travel, food, and warmth. When hitchhikers meet on the road, we tend to say a brief hello, then try to put some space between us as quickly as possible. Hoboes can ride two dozen in a boxcar, but two hitchhikers is the maximum number that will get any rides, and even then at least one of the two had better be a woman. Most of the committed, addicted, longtime hitchhikers travel alone, and even if we happen upon another longtime hitchhiker in a bar or campsite, we don't have much fellow feeling. We don't gather in herds or packs, and you can't spot a hitchhiker walking through town the way you can spot a railroad bum. For one thing, we tend to be clean, since a filthy hitchhiker won't get many rides. On the trains, dirt is unavoidable, and one good run will ruin you for the roadside until you can find a shower and a laundromat. For another, hitching and hoboing involve different views of the world. We each claim to be driven by a lust for freedom, but the freedoms are almost diametrical opposites: Hoboes can look and act any way they please, and can ride alone or with gangs of friends, and drink, sing, or even have sex as they roll across the country. They see places you cannot see from any road, unmarred by billboards and chain restaurants. They spend their lives in a separate world, a loose confederacy of loners and misfits held together by codes and habits, and the ostracism of the settled, property-owning townsfolk.

A train, though, goes its own way and follows its own schedule. Grab hold, and you are like Sinbad tied to the foot of the roc, watching the countryside pass but unable to do anything about it until the monster alights. If you spot an inviting beach or barbecue stand, a fairground or a waterfall, you can only gaze back at it and wait to see what is around the next curve. Or suppose you get stuck between trains? Heading east from Spokane, I ended up marooned for thirty-six hours in Glendive, Montana. I was traveling with another guy by then, and we were getting into the hobo mystique, so we waited it out. By the time a train finally came through, all the men working the yards knew us, and were happy to help us—or maybe just eager to get rid of us—so they promised to find something wrong with it that would keep it stopped for at least half an hour, giving us plenty of time to find a comfortable boxcar.

That was not a terrible experience, but no sane person would choose to spend a day and a half in Glendive. Drop me off there alone, clean, and trusting the road, and in at most a couple of hours I would be moving. If the weather was clear, I wouldn't even wait that long. I would start walking out of town, and if no one stopped for a few hours I would ramble along, a romantic dot on the prairie, under that immense Montana sky. And you rarely have to ramble very long. It is even easier to get rides when you are walking down a stretch of country road than when you are waiting in a town. You look like a clean-limbed, athletic hiker rather than a bored panhandler, and drivers get caught up in the romance of a lone figure striding along the highway.

Besides, if I had been hitchhiking, I might never have ended up in Glendive in the first place. There are only a half-dozen rail lines across the country, but there are hundreds of roads. If I hadn't been locked into the freight route, I might have ducked south along the Bitterroot River, through Yellowstone, or toward the Black Hills. Or I might have headed north into Canada. A hitchhiker can go anywhere that there's a road, and if that's not freedom enough, you can cut off on a footpath, hike through some open country, and catch another ride wherever and whenever you choose to intersect with civilization.

Like all the choices we make in our lives, it's a trade-off. The hoboes don't like to have to sit there with a driver, being polite and dependent. I know just how they feel, and there is a great freedom to lying in a boxcar, playing music, reading, watching the scenery, not having to conciliate or entertain anybody but yourself. And even the view through the windshield of a semi is nothing to the view you get sitting on top of a grain car, king of the moving mountain and lord of all you survey.

But let the weather turn ugly. I have huddled for warmth in the front of a boxcar, and being a writer and a romantic idiot I was pleased to file the experience away for future use, but as the night wore on the novelty faded and I imagined myself in a warm semi cab, watching the rain run down the windows. Stopping for coffee. That doesn't sound like much, but spend a cold night camped out on the front platform of a grain car and you begin to value the chance to stop for something hot. Trucks even have a bed right there in the cab—a lot of truckers prefer not to have a stranger sleeping in it, and most of the time I would rather be up front watching the road, but there it is.

So these days I stick to the road, and watch the trains roll past, and I play them a friendly tune. It's nice to know that they are there if you want them.

TOWNSPEOPLE

Riverboats, trains, the mythic Highway 61, and the ghost of Mark Twain—what more could a night's stopping place provide? No sooner asked than answered. Wandering for the third time down Hannibal's Main Street, I passed the pizza parlor and a couple of young guys, smoking on the bench outside, took note of my guitar.

"You play guitar?"

"Yes."

"Whadda you play?"

I ran down a standard blues line, an easy way to make an impression.

"Hey, you're pretty good. What the fuck are you doing here?"

"I was hitching towards Iowa City, and thought I'd see what Hannibal was like."

"Well, now you've seen it. There's nothing here."

His friend chimed in: "I'm just here for the summer. What a boring shit-hole."

The first guy was squat and heavyset, in torn jeans and a black leather jacket. The second was thin, with stringy blond hair, a silver stud in his eyebrow, and an early attempt at a beard. A girl joined them, chunky, with hennaed hair in pigtails, wearing a shapeless black dress and work boots. I played her a blues riff too. I was in no hurry, and they clearly were desperate for anything that would break the monotony of one more boring evening in a boring small town, where they were stuck until they were old enough to get the hell out.

The funny part was that they bored me. I had met them too many times before, in too many places, always bored with wherever they happened to be. But I figured I owed them a little entertainment, because if I wanted to be honest, they were more Tom Sawyer than I was. What was Twain's hero but a kid stuck in Hannibal, hanging out, at loose ends, eager for any whiff of the world beyond these neat houses and too-familiar streets? Maybe I wasn't punk or metal enough to fit my listeners' chosen fantasies, but at least I was a new face for five or ten minutes, until the novelty wore off. Then I asked them where I could get a meal and a beer, and left them smoking on their corner.

The dinner options were pretty limited, at least at that hour: There was the pizza parlor and a bar and grill. I wanted a beer, so opted for the latter, and as I walked through the door the sound system was playing blues slide guitar. "Look-a here, the entertainment has arrived!" A guy at the bar had spotted me, and was kidding around. "You gonna play for us?"

"Sure, no problem." I was going along with the joke, but it looked like the fish were running and I had the right fly. If everything went well, the meal would be free and I might even pick up a few bucks and a bed for the night. Best to hold back, though, and cast my line nice and easy. I propped my guitar by a table, where it was visible but not obviously aimed at anyone, set my pack beside it, and ordered a draft beer and the broiled catfish dinner plate. As I ate, the few customers drifted out, till it was just me, the waitress, and the owner. I complimented him on his taste in music, and he asked me what I played. He shut off the sound system, and I tore off a Delta slide piece. He was enthusiastically complimentary, and told me that if I wanted to stick around till the weekend he could get me a job; a friend of his had a club in Keokuk where I could make a couple hundred dollars. The waitress brought my bill. I paid it. The owner asked if I wanted another beer, got one for himself as well, and joined me at my table. He was from Texas, had never expected to end up in Hannibal, but here he was. Had been here twelve years and didn't seem to be going anywhere. Missed the music scene in Austin, though. Always picks up hitchhikers, no matter how ratty-looking they are. I asked him if people around here ride the freights. He said no, but that a couple of months ago there was one guy: "I was in back, putting out the garbage, and there was this old guy with a big beard and a rolled-up blanket slung over his shoulder—a real, honest-to-god hobo. I said hello to him, and he asked me if I had any work he could do in exchange for a meal. I told him he was welcome to come in and have a hamburger, but he said, 'Not unless you have some work for me.' So I gave him a broom and let him sweep the back lot. Then he ate his hamburger, and I guess he must have caught the next train out."

The classic taxonomy of American outcasts and wanderers: a hobo works and travels; a tramp travels but doesn't work; a bum neither works nor travels. The old man was a real hobo, in the classic style. They prefer the trains, but occasionally you see one out on the highway. They never hitch, though, either with thumb or sign; they just walk along the side of the road, never looking to see if a car is coming, willing to make their own way on foot if no one happens to pull over. There are some truck drivers who, passing me by as a rambling panhandler, will stop for those old men, respecting their pride and self-reliance and recognizing them as kindred spirits. Vanishing breeds, ancient codes, a nomadic aristocracy that collects no rents and prosecutes no wars, still making its rarely noticed way in an ever more alienating and hectic world.

It was past time for the restaurant to close. The waitress had gone home an hour ago. I had drunk my one free beer, paid for with one free song. No offer of a bed, and I had no taste for hinting, with the sky clear and full of stars and the spirit of Huck Finn and the hoboes watching over me. The Twain house was just across the way, its garden beckoning. The gate was even open, but a street light made that path too bright. Instead, I walked up the cobbled side street, ducked into an unlighted, empty parking lot that sat flush with the top of the garden's back wall, slid down among the trees, and spread my plastic poncho on a bed of thick, fresh pine needles.

SLEEPING ROUGH

How many rhapsodies have been written to the simple pleasures of a night under the stars, and how rare it has become. I grew up in a world of hiking and camping, but it was a puritan, citified world where one walked up mountains with a full pack, then pitched a nylon tent to shut out the night breezes and the sky. We carried all our food, cooked on folding propane stoves, then mummified ourselves in high-tech, synthetic-fiber sleeping bags.

When I first set out to be a rambling musician, I had all that camping equipment: a big frame pack, a sleeping bag, a canteen, and a solid wooden case for my guitar. It's a good thing I was young and strong. Over the years, objects got stolen or wore out, or I simply got tired of carrying them, and with every piece I left behind my life got easier. Now, my pack is about the size of the ones that kids take to school, my guitar hangs free on my shoulder, and I sleep out in whatever clothes I have. There are some nights when it would be nice to have a big, warm sleeping bag, but every day it is a pleasure not to be carrying one on my back, and even in cold climates you can sleep in a down jacket a lot better than you can walk in a down sleeping bag. As for a tent, if it rains I find shelter—a shed, an awning, the space under a porch, a child's plastic playhouse, the tarpaulin-covered deck of a moored sailboat—and when it isn't raining there is no reason to block out the sky with anything more than some fresh-smelling trees to keep off the morning dew.

That's how it always was in the books I read as a kid, but I guess I didn't have Tom Sawyer's good sense. I sometimes let myself be fooled into believing that the books were fiction and the adults around me were teaching fact, even when that led to such obvious silliness as carrying ten pounds of extra equipment to sleep out on a warm summer night. No one could tell Tom that respectable Hannibal was more real than the knights, damsels, and dashing outlaws in the storybooks, and he always opted for the romantic route. Me, I believed enough of the literature to run off and seek my fortune, and to enjoy some cold and hungry nights as spice to the adventure, but it took me years to learn that the ramblers in the stories were accurately and ideally equipped when they left home with nothing but a change of clothes and a lump of bread and cheese.

Of course, if you are headed across the Rockies in September, you need to carry more than you would to visit Georgia in July. So now I buttoned up my wool jacket and pulled a wool hat over my ears and an extra pair of socks onto my hands, and covered my legs with my down jacket, for when the cold set in. Then I lay on my back and gazed up through the branches, listening to the night sounds and feeling absurdly happy. All pleasures are in contrast, and tonight's were sweetened by the afternoon's doubts. Riding toward St. Louis, I had got to thinking that I was too old for this life, that while it wasn't truly hard or dangerous, it had ceased to be much fun. And here I was, a few short hours, a river, and a freight train later, loving it as much as I ever had. Why had I even briefly thought of angling for a place on someone's musty couch, when I was in Mark Twain country? Petty crimes that hurt no one are part of the spice of life, and I was trespassing on sacred ground with as much pleasure and as light a conscience as Tom or Huck had hooking apples.

My mind drifted off to previous literary resting places: The evening a friend and I snuck our packs into the stone cellars of Hamlet's castle in Elsinore, Denmark, only to find that at closing time the guards sent a dog to sniff out just our sort of illicit romantics. Or, more successfully, the night that, walking through Normandy with a thin sheaf of Shakespeare's histories in my pack, I found myself at sunset unexpectedly arrived at Agincourt, and read King Henry's exhortation to his troops by flashlight, stretched out in the middle of the battlefield. A well-chosen or serendipitous sleeping place is one of the great joys of travel. I've slept in the center of a Paleolithic stone circle on Orkney, and been woken by a chorus of unseen singers walking past the thicket where I had hidden myself beside a field in Botswana. And then there have been all the nights by various highways, soothed rather than troubled by the growl of passing engines.

Tonight, there was only the rustle of branches and the crickets, and once or twice a rumbling, clanking freight. Human Hannibal was fast asleep, safe in its historic houses. Pleased with my luck and the day's travels, I curled myself into a cozy ball and slept the sleep of the just.

THE TRAMP'S
ALARM CLOCK

The night air was soothing, and I was tired enough to take full advantage. I slept lightly, though, as one does outdoors, so I noticed immediately when soft voices followed a flashlight beam in at the gate. There were two of them, and they walked along the raised wooden path leading to the door of the museum. "Over there, in the trees," one said, and the flashlight beam played across the ground, back and forth. I kept still, but eventually it must have caught the glint of my poncho or the guitar. "There he is!" I sat up as they walked toward me, keeping both my hands in view. They were police, of course.

"What are you doing here?"

That was an easy one. "Sleeping."

"We saw the gate was open. You came in through there?"

"No, actually I came over this wall from the parking lot."
Stupid twists of fate; I should have closed the gate.

"Can we see some ID?"

"Of course."

They called my license number in, and waited for a response.
Perfectly polite, just doing their job. Still, they would have to
move me on. "This is private property. You can't stay here. If you
need a place to sleep, there's a place called Hope House and they'll
give you a bed."

"Actually, I have enough money for a motel. But it was a warm
night, and I came here because I've read a lot of Mark Twain, and
I asked myself, 'What would Tom Sawyer do?'"

The cop nodded; not friendly, not unfriendly, all in a night's
work. "I understand. Now pick up your stuff, and I'm going to
watch you walk out of here."

I already had my poncho folded and my down jacket packed
in its stuff sack. "No problem. Could you just shine your flashlight
around here to make sure I haven't dropped anything?"

He was a decent guy, and played the beam over my erstwhile
campsite. Then I shouldered my pack and walked up the hill to
the highway, crossed it, climbing over the cement divider, and
walked until a sign said I was half a mile from Route 61. It was a
lovely night for walking, and since I wanted to get an early start in
the morning I had no complaints about catching my last few hours
of sleep nearer the main road. I was only half awake, and moved

slowly, nurturing my drowsiness. There was a strip of woods up a slight hill to the right, and I found a break in the highway fence and wriggled through. More pines, taller than in town. The lower branches of a bushy fir make a natural tent, and I found one that was perfect, curled up under it, and comfortably slept away the last couple of hours until dawn.

MIDTOWN CROSSROADS

I woke at first light and walked out to Highway 61. The morning was gray and chilly, and I went into a gas station mini-mart and got a cup of coffee. There were two gas stations, side by side, and they were the only places where cars would be able to pull over for me. I was in the middle of the "golden mile," the prefab main street that had replaced old Hannibal. Four lanes of traffic, no sidewalks or breakdown lanes. The only good news was that there was a stoplight just before the stations, so cars would be moving slowly and drivers could see me and have time to pull in. I didn't see much chance of a truck stopping. There were quite a few on the road, but it would take an unusually sympathetic and determined driver to be willing to block a whole lane of traffic just to pick up a lousy hitchhiker.

On balance, there were good points and bad points to the situation: Early morning is a good time for hitching, but it is always hard to get a ride in the middle of a town. There is something inappropriate about standing in a business district with your thumb out; it's like wearing a down jacket in the summer—you're not doing any harm, but it looks peculiar. It is also discouraging for the hitchhiker, because there are hundreds of cars passing, but almost all of them are just going somewhere else in town. You try to sort them as they pass: The school buses are obvious, and so are the parents chauffeuring children. Women applying lipstick at the light are presumably on their way to work.

All the cars had Missouri license plates, except a couple from Illinois, implying that there was very little long-range traffic. A pickup passed, three men crowded in the front, gardening equipment in the back. A phone company van, probably the same one that had passed half an hour earlier.

An old man with a cane, walking slowly and carefully, came out of a little alley by the first gas station and went into the mini-mart. He came out a few minutes later, and walked over to me.

"Been here long?"

"No, just a half hour or so."

"Where you from?"

"Boston."

"Huh. You hitchhike from there?"

"Yeah. It's been going fine."

"Well, at least you've got a nice morning for it. Long as you're not in a hurry."

"Nope. Just heading up to Iowa City."

"Well, good luck then."

A couple of kids came out of the same alley and passed within a few feet of me, pretending not to look, whispering and giggling. By now it was full daylight. I was tempted to walk out to the edge of town, but I had no way of knowing how far that might be, and there was no place where cars would be able to stop once I left the gas stations. A ten-minute walk might put me in a much better spot, but it was equally possible that I might waste twenty minutes walking, unable to hitch, without improving my situation. At least it would be a change. I don't mind waiting for an hour or two on a quiet country road, but it gets annoying when you are at a gas station in an urban business strip, watching a constant stream of useless local traffic. I had been there forty-five minutes by now. Let the gods decide: at one hour, if I was still there, I'd start walking.

I waited, thumb out, automatic smile on my face, for another fifteen minutes. Then, as the second hand on my watch reached twelve, I shouldered my pack, turned my back on the oncoming traffic, and a car pulled up alongside me. The driver stuck his head out the window: "I saw you on my way over to Wal-Mart, and I said to myself, 'If he's still there when I get done, I'll give him a lift.'"

OF GRAIN ELEVATORS

AND SKYDIVING

My rescuer was a tall, broad-shouldered man with a scruffy Abe Lincoln beard, a lazy smile, and bright, lively eyes. He said he was only going about twenty miles, up to the Quincy turnoff, and he could either take me to the split or drop me at a gas station that was a regular stopping place for truckers. I said I was fine with whichever he thought was better; he knew the area, and it didn't really matter once I was out of town. He said he would normally be happy to take me a few miles further, but he was already late for work. He traveled all over the region, inspecting grain elevators, and had to get to the office and pick up the day's schedule. He didn't know where he'd be sent, but if it was up 61 and I was still there, he would pick me up again. We passed a cleared field with a big metal shed at one end, and he said they used to have a skydiving school there. He asked if I'd ever jumped. I said I preferred to stay on terra firma, and as the old joke has it, "De more firma, de less terra."

"I know what you mean; I was always scared of heights myself. But a few years ago I was over in Illinois with a buddy of mine who used to be a paratrooper, and we were drinking, and he bet me if I tried it I would never want to do anything else. So I said what the hell, and the next morning he brought me over here and we hired a plane. And he was right. I loved it, and when my oldest son turned eighteen I took him up for a birthday present, and I did the same with my daughter. She had to wait a year, because they'd closed the field here by that time, but we were on vacation in Texas, down near the border, and I found a place down there. So I took her up for her nineteenth birthday. She'd never been in a plane in her life, and she jumped right out. She's got balls, that one. So I've got one more son to go; he turns eighteen next year."

"It's kind of like birds, pushing the babies out of the nest."

He liked that: "Yeah, and you know, it worked. Both of the older kids have gone off out of state and set themselves up in their own places."

It makes sense. Jumping out of an airplane gives you a sense of accomplishment and self-confidence, a feeling that you can do anything if you just screw up your nerve and take that crazy leap. In a way, it is like hitchhiking across the United States. I wondered if he would recommend that his kids try that as well. An odd thought: If I got up in a room full of sensible adults and suggested that it would be good for all young people to try skydiving, they might think me a bit odd, but few would consider me dangerous. Yet if I get up in the same room and advocate hitchhiking, a lot of people get nervous and even angry. Do they really think that getting into a stranger's car is that much more hazardous than jumping out of an airplane? Most of them did some hitching in their youth and tend to recall the experience with nostalgia, and few have ever donned a parachute. Or is their real fear that, while they know their sons and daughters have better sense than to jump out of a plane, they worry that some might actually listen to me and get out on the nearest highway? Sadly, I have no such expectations. Young people have been so pounded by reports about the violence, hate, and danger in the world around them that very few will ever consider trusting their lives to the kindness of a random motorist. But anyone who takes reassurance in that fact should think long and hard about what it means, for them and for us, and for the future of humanity. I am glad for my driver's children that they were brave enough to trust their lives to some nylon webbing, a silk canopy, and the intangible buoyancy of air—but I wish I could assume they would feel safer on solid earth, in the company of a helpful stranger like their dad.

We passed the gas station the driver had mentioned, but he didn't stop. Then we went on past the Quincy turnoff. "I'm in a hurry, but this isn't a good place to stop, so I'll take you a little further up the road." A half mile on, the road straightened out, with a breakdown lane and plenty of visibility. He pulled over and dropped me off, waving good-bye as he made an illegal U-turn over the brown dirt median strip and headed off to work.

THE EASY LIFE

Now that I was out on an empty stretch of road, miles from anywhere, I naturally became aware that I hadn't eaten any breakfast. Another stupid habit, developed in my youth. But, like sleeping rough, going without food is proof that your body can take the life, and given the right attitude, hunger can be invigorating. The next town was seven miles down the road, so if no one picked me up I could walk there in less than two hours. It was the first time this trip that I was somewhere I could walk. For a hitchhiker, that's a pretty fair definition of "country": a stretch of road where you might as well be walking as standing in a good spot. This was not a particularly scenic bit of country. It was flat and dust-yellow, and there was some kind of electrical plant or generator over to the right. I stepped around the corpse of a dead piglet, a new addition to the long catalog of roadkill met in similar circumstances. I've always liked the periods of walking, as long as the weather cooperates. It makes a change from riding, a chance to stretch your legs, and there's also the macho pleasure of covering ground under your own steam. That's one pleasure that grows with age, the enjoyment of pushing your body, going hungry, sleeping on bare ground, then shouldering a pack and walking ten or fifteen miles if you have to.

Also, it was an opportunity to yodel. Set me out in the middle of the prairie and I can sing like Jimmie Rodgers, especially if there's no one for miles around. It had been over a year, and the flat farmland roofed by a cloudless blue sky formed a perfect concert hall:

I may be rough, I may be wild,
I may be tough and accounted vile,
But I can't give up my good old rough and rowdy ways
Yodel-ay-ee-hoo, de-lay-ee-hoo, de-lay-eeee . . .

I was kind of disappointed when a car pulled over. It was a big, white Lincoln Town Car, and the driver was a heavyset old guy with glasses, a snap-brim hat, and a thick, white moustache. He was a retired car salesman. "Would you believe I bought this car at auction for under a thousand dollars? She just needed new tires on her and new shocks. I have a Suburban at home I got for seven thousand, but I'm thinking I might just sell it, this one rides so easy." He had given up the business a few years ago and was living on social security, but still dealt here and there, under the table, just to keep his hand in.

I commented on the good weather. "It's not good for people around here," he said. "Look at that field of little bitty corn. Didn't grow up into anything, and even that's burnt to hell. We got a lot of rain last week, but that was the first we've had in months. It might save some of the beans, but it's too late for the corn."

It wasn't just the weather that troubled him. "I'm glad I'm not young these days; it's getting too hard to make a living. It used to be easy, you could do just about anything and get by. Not get rich, but you could have a place and feed your family. I didn't go to school for anything in particular, just did this and that, and drifted into the car business. These days, there's no easy way to make a living, so I think the best thing is to find something you enjoy doing." He nodded toward my guitar.

It is one of the oddities of hitchhiking, how many drivers seem to admire or envy you for being out on the road, by yourself, with no visible ties to anything. It is the other American dream, the flip side of the good job, the house in the suburbs, the spouse and 2.4 kids. And it has the added allure of being within reach, something they might grab hold of if things were just a little different. I once had a millionaire pick me up and spend our whole drive talking about how much he wished he could get out on the road like I was doing. He only interrupted the fantasy to draw my attention to a cherry red sports car: "I've got three other cars, and that Porsche that just passed us, did you see the girl inside? That's my mistress, she's a modern dancer. I have a factory making directional systems for guided missiles, I could give you a job tomorrow—but you wouldn't want that, would you? You have a better life than I have. I wish I could just pack it all in and join you."

I used to think those wistful monologues were pure bullshit. I would listen politely, but I felt like saying, "No, you don't really want to get out here on the road. Because if you did, you'd do it." I was wrong, though, or at least unfair. Because I was lucky from the beginning. I didn't have parents who needed me to support them, I never had kids, and the first woman I proposed to turned me down flat. I don't need a stable income, and what I do need I can make as a musician and writer. So it's easy for me to pull up stakes and hit the road when the mood strikes me. And yes, other people can too, almost any of them if they want it badly enough, but it is not always such an easy decision. I have met guys on the road who have abandoned families—a couple of women, too, but mostly men—or whose parents haven't spoken to them in twenty years and may be alive or dead. And they don't talk about the freedom as lightly. They talk about how they were trapped, how they really had no choice, and they may have a fierce joy about them, but also the sense that if they were better men they might have stuck it out and fulfilled their responsibilities.

For most people, though, the responsibilities are beside the point. If they think about it seriously for even a minute, they are perfectly conscious that they would not want this life. They like knowing where they will wake up tomorrow, and have no real desire to sleep in backyards and be rousted by cops at four in the morning. You have to be a little strange to enjoy that. But I'm glad that they at least like to toy with the idea. It is a kind of reassurance for me, implying that I am not completely and inexplicably nuts. And of course, the vicarious sense of freedom they get from picking up a roadside wanderer gives them another good reason to pull over.

My current driver told me he had once hitched home from North Dakota with his ex-wife. They'd gone up there to deliver a pickup truck, and were going to take a bus back, but they were having breakfast in a diner full of truck drivers, and he decided to ask around. He found a guy heading south, and after that they were passed from truck to truck, the drivers arranging the rides over the CB. He shook his head, smiling at the memory. "That woman was a lot of fun. She was game for anything. And I really enjoyed that trip. Now, I got diabetes and heart trouble, and I need a cane just to get from the front door to my car. I'm all old and beat to shit."

He had planned to turn off earlier, heading west to the small town where he lived, but took me another ten miles up to Wayland, just a few miles from the state border. He said that would be a good place for me, because the truckers would all be taking a little branch road due north from there, the shortcut into Iowa.

OF TOLL BRIDGES

AND TORTS

Aside from the truck turnoff, Wayland did not have much to recommend it. I was on what seemed to be the main street, but could not see even a corner store where I might buy an apple or a box of crackers. The small Midwestern town is a vanishing species, its descendents nothing but clusters of houses that still call themselves a town even though their residents have to drive five miles to buy a pack of cigarettes. Wal-Mart and its ilk have left a swath of destruction that neatly complements the effects of a neutron bomb: the radiation kills people but leaves property intact; the malls leave the people, but destroy the town. I would have to do without breakfast.

I walked half a mile to where the shortcut headed north. A sign said there was a toll bridge in four miles, and I set off walking down neat streets lined with small, tidy houses. In the first two blocks two trucks passed, and it occurred to me that I would probably have a better chance of getting a ride if I went back to the turnoff, where they had to stop. Experience was teaching me that I needn't plan any four-mile walks, at least on a sunny day in this part of the country. So I ambled back to the corner, set my pack down by a telephone pole, and sang a couple more Jimmie Rodgers numbers. Then another truck appeared, slowed for the turn, stopped, and the driver waved me to climb in.

He was about thirty, with short hair, a neatly clipped moustache, and a soul patch under his lip. He was going into Burlington to make a delivery, but then would go on home to Cedar Rapids, so if I didn't mind waiting an hour he could drop me on the highway outside Iowa City. The way the hitching was going, I said he could just drop me wherever he turned off for Burlington. From there it would only be another fifty miles, and I would probably be in Iowa City before he was out of Burlington. He agreed that would be quicker for me, adding that he picks people up pretty often and they don't seem to have much trouble getting rides around here. He drives this route a lot, just short hauls: "I'm never out more than three days—just long enough for my wife to get to missing me, but not long enough for her to get pissed off." They had been together since ninth grade, and he talked about her like a good buddy. She was one of his two true loves, her and his motorbike. Pretty soon, she might have him to herself: "They're talking about passing a helmet law, and if that happens I may just have to quit riding. I don't like them telling me what to do, making laws for my own protection. If I'm not hurting anybody else, it should be my own choice what I do."

We came to the toll bridge, a two-lane affair with a single booth in the center and a hand-lettered sign on its wall: Cars 50¢/Semis $2. The toll taker was a skinny old farmer, and he and the truck driver exchanged friendly hellos. As we drove on, the trucker explained that the old guy owned the bridge; it is one of the last private toll bridges in the United States. He farms as well, and owns the land on both sides of the river. His father established the toll and he inherited it, and they just won a five-year court battle with the government, who had argued that the bridge was public property. The question will eventually be moot, since a new highway is being built, but meanwhile he has a few more years of business. Iowa has already built a four-lane to the river bank, a few hundred yards west of the bridge, but Missouri has budget problems and is way behind schedule. "Guy must do OK, with all the traffic comes up this way." The driver approved of individual initiative. Big government and over-regulation were ruining the country. Which brought us back to the helmet law and the high insurance rates his boss had to deal with. "It's all the lawsuits. Like that McDonald's case, the lady whose coffee was too hot. If the coffee'd been cold, she would have complained about that."

I considered making a case for universal health coverage, so people wouldn't have to bring lawsuits to pay their medical bills, but a smart hitchhiker keeps his mouth shut about politics and religion unless specifically questioned. Not that my views would have necessarily been any different from his, or would have pissed him off, but it's not my place. He is holding up his side of the bargain by giving me a ride, and I hold up mine by making him feel good about it, so he'll pick up more hitchhikers in the future. If a driver wants my opinion, he'll ask for it. And they rarely do. Talkative drivers pick you up because they feel like talking, and quiet drivers like to drive quietly. So you listen and make encouraging noises, or you shut up and watch the scenery. Either way, it's their call. This driver was talkative, but not annoying: I didn't agree with everything he said, but he wasn't railing on about "niggers" and "towel-heads" and "the future of the white race," or boasting about all the hookers at the truck stops who give it away to him for free because he's so good. He was just a decent guy trying to live his life with as little hassle as possible. So I said "uh-huh" a lot and nodded when he glanced my way, and after another half hour he dropped me at the Burlington off-ramp.

OF AIR CONDITIONERS
AND CONSPIRACY

I was on a limited-access highway again, but in Iowa you can hitch even on the interstates, so I wasn't worried about legal problems. I was going to walk ahead to the on-ramp, where I could get both the highway traffic and any new arrivals, but as it turned out I had another ride before I could even get my pack onto my shoulders. It was a white pickup, liberally spattered with mud, and the driver got out and hurried around to my side. He was white-haired, with a jerky, distracted manner, and he opened the passenger door and began rummaging inside. "Just give me a second to clear out the front," he said over his shoulder. "I'm late already, but I stopped because no one will pick you up these days."

I wasn't about to argue, and anyway he wasn't paying attention to me. He was clearing tools and electrical gizmos and wires off the floor and seat, and tossing them into the truck bed, which was already a mass of disordered junk. I added my pack to the pile, keeping my guitar with me, and we were off.

He was headed for Cedar Rapids, to repair a woman's air conditioner. He was already an hour late. The air conditioner was new, but she said it had been installed wrong. He had told her to call the same guys who installed it and get them to come back and do it right, but she didn't trust them. He does all kinds of electrical repairs, and whatever else people need done, a jack of all trades. He used to hitchhike himself. He's from Keokuk, lived there all his life. "Except sometimes I just had to bust out. I'd get mad as hell about something, take all my money out of the bank and hitch out to California. I'm a handyman, so I could always find work, wherever I was. I did that five or six times. Just got mad and took off. I could've drove my car, I had one, but then I'd just've had to pay for gas and everything, and I wanted my money to last as long as it could. I wouldn't tell nobody I was going, I'd just clear out. But you can't do that anymore these days, 'cause nobody'd pick you up."

I didn't tell him how easily the rides had been coming. A lot of drivers take pleasure in rescuing you from dire straits, and are disappointed if you tell them you were only waiting a couple of minutes. Though, to be fair, this one didn't seem to care much one way or the other; he just liked to talk.

"Where you from?" he asked me.

"Boston."

"You live in Boston? OK, OK. That's near the Kennedys, isn't it?"

I expected the anti-Kennedy rant—a southern specialty, but available across the country—but instead it was the full-bore conspiracy rant. And my driver was no armchair amateur. He had gone down to Dallas and interviewed one of the two cops who had been riding beside JFK's car. And he had all the details at his fingertips: The Federal Reserve bank was the evil genius behind it all, with Johnson playing along and the CIA handling the dirty work. Richard Helms was the point man. "Do you know anything about the Federal Reserve? Hell, nobody does. It's a so-called private bank, but really it's just four guys in a room, and they lend money to the government at four point five percent, but it's not backed up by anything, it's all just paper. JFK was going to put the government's finances on solid ground, he was going to issue new government notes backed up by gold and silver. The day Johnson took office, he killed that plan dead. You scratch my back, I'll scratch yours. Helms was just a regular agent before that, and he was made director of the CIA. Did you know that all of them met on November nineteen at the book depository? Oswell never even fired his gun. He was working for the CIA, but they set him up . . ." And so on.

I was drowsing off, but managed to make vaguely appropriate noises. He had piles of documents at home, was talking to experts on both coasts. He'd like to take me into Iowa City, but he was already two hours late and the lady was gonna give him hell, so he'd drop me off at the exit and I could catch a bus or something into town. What was the name of the guy who killed Oswell? (He kept calling him "Oswell," not Oswald.)

"Jack Ruby," I said, to show I was paying attention.

"Yeah, they got him too. Johnson was there in Texas, just three days before the assassination, him and Helms met up there. People just don't know this stuff."

He turned off at the Iowa City exit. "I'd better take you on in. I'm so late already, another ten minutes won't make a difference. She can't get no madder than she is already." He dropped me in the center of town, and I found a pay phone and called my friends.

A HISTORICAL

INVESTIGATION

One of the joys of travel is the savor it gives to not traveling. After fifteen hundred miles of rolling from car to truck to car to truck, and sleeping where I could, it was a luxury to get off the road for a couple of days, eat regular meals, sleep in a bed, and take advantage of the college-town amenities by strolling quiet streets, lounging in cafes, and browsing my way through secondhand bookstores. It was a chance to relax and ponder, and to add some balance to my journey by putting hitchhiking in a broader context. One trip across the country is, after all, only a narrow window on a wide world, and my experience is only one of many. So before we head out across the great plains and up into the Rockies, let us likewise get off the road for a few chapters, and broaden our perspective by surveying some history and exploring the lore and conditions that underlie this venture.

As both word and concept, hitchhiking is of quite recent vintage, but its roots lie far deeper. Splitting the word into its component parts, *hitch* dates back at least to the fifteenth century, and apparently derives from the Middle English *icchen*, "to move as with a jerk, to stir." By the late sixteenth century, this word had taken on a secondary meaning, "to become fastened by a hook," and most authorities trace *hitchhiking* along this branch, speculating that sleds were hitched to horses, then riders to drivers. Another derivation, which strikes me as more probable, is suggested by the listing in Noah Webster's 1841 *Dictionary of the English Language*: "To move by jerks, or with stops; as, in colloquial language, to hitch along." As for hike, it can be traced back to the early nineteenth century, and almost certainly is far older. It was found in English rural dialects, and in its early print transcriptions appears as *haik* or *hyke*, meaning "to walk vigorously." Exactly when these two words were combined is not clear, but in its modern sense, *hitchhiking* seems to have gained currency only in the late teens of the twentieth century.

Indeed, I can't see how it could have emerged any earlier. Before the motorcar became ubiquitous, while we can point to examples of what might now be considered hitching, they were incidents of travel rather than a chosen mode unto themselves. This was because, with rare exceptions, travelers in earlier times encountered no speedier means of locomotion than their own legs. It is a charming fallacy to cast ourselves back to another age and imagine that we are all knights and ladies, of whatever culture, the sort of people whose journeys are related in old tales and plays, or painted on the walls of tombs and temples, mounted on fast chargers, elephants, or slave-oared barques—or in later and more prosaic years as passengers in stagecoaches, picking up fresh horses at each inn to speed us on our way. The truth is, most lone travelers in the past had neither horse nor carriage. They walked, and if they chanced from time to time to catch a ride on a friendly farm wagon, this rested their feet but did not increase their speed.

Travel was slow, but that did not mean that it was limited in scope or variety. Walk four hours in the morning and four in the afternoon, and in one summer you can cross the United States, from New York to Los Angeles. It would not be a pleasant, easy trip, but only because so much of the terrain acquired its human amenities in the age of modern transportation, leaving great stretches of land where you cannot find even a drink of water. Make the same trip in most of Europe, Africa, Asia, or South America—anywhere but the bleakest deserts, thickest jungles, or most forbidding mountain ranges—and you will find a town appearing whenever you would choose to pause, that being the principle on which the towns were founded. Moving slowly, you will pick up local languages, note subtle changes of landscape, and, unburdened by the need for wide and solid roads, wander where no car has penetrated. Given sound legs and sufficient time, you can range the length of continents.

We will never know how many travelers once walked the roads and pathways of the earth, carrying only their clothes and maybe a musical instrument, with no particular goal or reason except the constant pleasure of changing scenes and people. The few narratives that have survived come either from the precious minority who could write or from the handful of distinguished persons whose deeds were deemed by court or church historians to warrant preservation. (Marco Polo was a rare exception: we have his story because he happened to be tossed in jail alongside a writer, who transcribed his memoirs.) Far and away the greater part of ancient, footloose wanderers left no record of their multivalent perambulations. But time and again, when the historically hallowed travelers arrived in distant and exotic climes, they found that other, unnamed visitors had been there first. Vagabonds are as old as humanity, since there has never been a time when people—few, perhaps, but always there—did not burn with curiosity to know what lay beyond the furthest mountain they could see, and having found that out, beyond the mountain after that.

What forever altered the population of the public highways was the arrival of the automobile, the first mass-produced, cheap, fast form of transportation. How recent this arrival really is, and what changes it has made, are hard for most of us to comprehend. We tend to think of cars as an integral part of the Industrial Revolution, and when we imagine a carless world, to think of rural hamlets, with horse-drawn wagons making their way between open fields and small, neat cottages. But my father grew up on a crowded apartment block in Brooklyn, New York City, and on the next block there was a fire station with horses that, when the alarm would ring, came thundering magnificently down his street, towing the clattering pumps. Today, that urban memory seems as ancient as Ben Jonson's London, but as I browsed through the used-book racks I stumbled on a volume titled *Scenic America*, which took me back to that lost world. A photographic survey compiled around 1900, it had a picture of

Pittsburgh, with a caption explaining that what had once been known as the "Smoky City" because of its coal-fired factories was now powered by clean, natural gas, and known as the "Iron City." A panoramic view from Mount Washington showed an industrial metropolis little different from the downtown as it is today, but the only land-based vehicles were public streetcars. Flipping to other pages, I found photos of New York, Washington, Boston, San Francisco, and Main Street in Los Angeles. There was traffic everywhere, on foot, on rails, or pulled by horses—but not a single automobile.

Even a hundred years later, those of us who live in downtown areas can conduct virtually all our business as people did back then. I know plenty of New Yorkers who would not consider owning a car. Outside the cities, though, the world has been utterly transformed. And yet, even in the countryside it took some decades before cars became a universal mode of travel. In the 1920s and on through the Depression, one could still find people making long journeys on foot, and if they got a ride it was often in a slow farm truck rather than a Model T. As long as cars were rare and relatively expensive novelties, it was hard to thumb a lift in one, since any driver who was willing to take passengers tended to have the seats full of neighbors and relatives from the moment the motor was sparked, even if they were just touring around the block. Today, in less technologically developed or cash-poor countries, it is still like that: if someone from a village is driving into town, the car is full of friends who have seized the opportunity to do their shopping or just to go along for the proverbial ride. In India or Africa, I rode only with the wealthy and the truckers, and had I not been a rare, white foreigner, the wealthy would have passed me by without a glance and the truckers would have demanded a fare. Alas, even free rides are distributed unequally in this world, and "them that's got shall get" remains the rule for footsore travelers.

True hitchhiking is thus a relatively recent arrival, born of the confluence of disposable income and mass production. The earliest evidence of a full-fledged hitching trip dates only to 1910, when an English writer and photographer named Tickner Edwardes (author of *The Lore of the Honey-bee*) published a book called *Lift-Luck on Southern Roads*. In the introduction, Edwardes emphasized the novelty of his mode of travel:

> The journey covers . . . some two hundred odd miles, through five southern counties, and was conceived on an unusual plan. For I went neither on foot, nor by any of the wonted means of conveyance beloved of tourists; neither by motor, nor cycle, phaeton nor ambling nag. . . . I got me, to tell the truth, through the whole two-hundred-mile stretch of the way, with camera and pack on shoulder and at surprisingly little expense, by means of Lifts, taken in any chance vehicle that might be faring in my direction.

Although his journey took place during the heyday of early motor travel, only one of Edwardes's "Lifts" was in a standard automobile, and it was so terrifyingly fast that he vowed never to accept another. In general, he rode in horse-drawn wagons, and the exceptions make up an odd assemblage: he jolted downhill on the side-step of a parson's bicycle, covered four miles in the back seat of a postman's tricycle, spent a drowsy afternoon on the tailboard of a "pantechnicon-van"—no description is given, but it apparently was slow and relaxing—and had a deafening ride perched on the coal bunker of a steam-driven traction engine.

The first evidence of a hitchhiker on this side of the Atlantic comes two years after Edwardes's pioneering volume, and though its hero was far more dependent on motor traffic, he accepted this fact only grudgingly. In the summer of 1912, the poet Vachel Lindsay set out from Illinois to New Mexico, proselytizing for his "Gospel of Beauty." His intention was to make the trip on foot, and the letters he wrote home drip with contempt for the vacationing families who whizzed past him, blind to the scenery he drank up at a sober pace. And yet, the modern age had brought temptations to which even a prophet would succumb: "About five o'clock in the evening some man making a local trip is apt to come along alone," Lindsay wrote. "He it is that will offer me a ride and spin me along from five to twenty-five miles before supper. This delightful use that may be made of an automobile in rounding out a day's walk has had something to do with mending my prejudice against it, despite the grand airs of the tourists that whirl by at midday. I still maintain that the auto is a carnal institution, to be shunned by the truly spiritual, but there are times when I, for one, get tired of being spiritual."

Lindsay's annoyance at the speeding tourists was an affectation as modern as the tourists themselves, since in a lot of areas the roads on which they could "whirl by" were not yet laid. Just nine years earlier, Horatio Nelson Jackson had taken sixty-three days to make the first automobile crossing of the United States, and when Lindsay made his walk one still could not traverse the continent on a paved surface. That breakthrough came the following year, with the completion of the Lincoln Highway, which traced the path of what is now I-80 from New York to San Francisco. Once the road was there, the cars were quick to follow—and with them the pioneering, long-haul hitchhikers. By 1916, the cross-country driving record had fallen to five days, and in 1921 a man named J. K. Christian won membership in the Chicago Adventurer's Club by hitching 3,023 miles in less than a month.

Did Christian call his mode of travel "hitchhiking"? I have no solid evidence one way or the other, but it seems likely. That he considered it a mode of travel suggests that it would have a name, and within another two years that name had appeared in print— not a surprising time lag for a slang term. The etymological inquiry remains unfinished, but *hitchhiking* was probably in common usage, at least in some parts of America, by the late teens. Indeed, the word may have predated the practice. The Texas guitarist and singer Mance Lipscomb, born in 1895, recalled that in his childhood they said they were "hitchhiking" when they hopped a freight train: "People call hitchhike thumbin' a ride with cars now," he told his biographer in the 1970s. "But we knowed about hitchhikin' wayyyy back in years, but we called it hitchhikin' on a train."

The supposition that, by the teens, the word was being used in its modern sense is circumstantially supported by the appearance of a parallel neologism in Britain. When Tickner Edwardes titled his book "Lift-Luck," he was using a term whose pedigree reached back two hundred years. In 1711, Jonathan Swift wrote in his *Journal to Stella* of how he was saving himself carriage fare: "I walked away sixpennyworth, and came within a shilling length, and then took a coach, and got a lift back for nothing." Charles Dickens and George Eliot both used *lift* in this sense, and it continues to be common today, though usually for a ride given by a friend rather than an anonymous roadside solicitation. During

World War I, though, the British roads were crowded for the first time both with soldiers in need of transportation and with motorized cargo vehicles. It was logical that the former would seize upon the latter, and H. L. Mencken reports that by 1915 the British lexicographer Eric Partridge had noted a new item of military slang: "lorry-hopping" or "lorry-jumping."

In America the distances were greater and the trucks more numerous, so there is every reason to assume the same solution was worked out, and that, come Armistice Day, there were thousands of soldiers hitchhiking across the country and calling the practice by its present name. It is a peculiarity of the historical record, though, that while trucks remain the classic long-haul ride, the earliest American equivalents of the British "lorry-hoppers" to leave their mark on the printed page were all hopping into private cars.

The first use of "hitchhiking" that survives in print is in the *Nation* magazine of September 19, 1923. A regular columnist who styled himself "The Drifter" reported that he had been driving through Vermont when he was hailed by three young women "hitch-hikers" en route from New York to Montreal. When he questioned them about their mode of travel, the most voluble of the trio answered, "There are thousands of us . . . We know girls who have hitched all the way to California. There's little trouble and most motorists are pretty good to us. It's a great way of seeing the country."

The Drifter was exultant at the notion of highways populated by "dryads" cadging lifts, but two months later the *Nation* ran an answering column by a more experienced and less romantic figure, "The Hiker": "HITCH-HIKING is no thoughtless expression of the untrammeled pioneer," he wrote, "but one of the most desolate of the exact sciences. . . . It takes a quick eye to appraise a car and its occupants before it has passed forever—whether one had best appeal to the driver or to the woman (or in these days man) beside him or her, how much room there is behind, and whether one had best ask a lift only to the next village or admit that one has fifty miles to go. Like all sciences it seems fascinating to the amateur, but it becomes dull and disappointing after a little experience."

Most writers being romantics, The Hiker's position was rarely echoed, then or later. When the Glasgow *Herald* printed a note from "an American correspondent" in 1927, advising that hitchhikers—"the latest curiosity born out of the linguistic genius of the Yankee"—were rivaling hoboes as knights of the road, it echoed the scientific note, writing that "the importuning of the motorist is evidently a highly organised and skilful business." However, it found the expertise more admirable than off-putting, adding that "There are apparently hitchhikers in the United States, who boast they can travel 500 miles free of charge without walking more than 10."

With the onset of the Depression, the roads became more crowded than ever. Though a flood of hobo narratives continued to canonize freight-hopping as the sine qua non of zero-budget travel, even Woody Guthrie at times was forced to stick out his thumb. He did not find the experience an undiluted pleasure—in his autobiography, *Bound for Glory*, he is forced to turn from sign painting to music after a driver absconds with his oils and brushes—but for some of his fellow travelers the highways brought notable advantages. Richard Wormser, a historian of hobo life, has written that, while male hoboes were more comfortable on the freights, many of the vagrant "road girls" preferred hitching: "They felt that men who owned cars were generally a better class of people than tramps that rode trains. It was fairly easy for a young girl to get a ride. It was also easier to control the situation. A man who had to keep his hands on the wheel of a car going forty miles an hour was far more manageable than a man or group of men sitting in a boxcar on a train and set on having sexual relations."

Wormser's observation is worth noting in our more paranoid times, since it is easy to forget how many women once found cheerful adventure on the roadside. The Drifter's Vermont dryads exemplified a generation of Jazz Age voyageuses, and while some were only casual travelers, the hitching bug bit women as strongly as it did men. Many traveled with their husbands or boyfriends, like the couples caught in photographs by Dorothea Lange and Walker Evans, but others chose to strike out in female pairs or trios or on their own. In 1946, the *New York Times* would report that a nineteen-year-old named Linda Folkard had been crowned "Miss Hitchhiker" for that year after completing a journey of fifteen thousand miles, while on the other side of the globe, the Australian Pioneer Women's Hall of Fame includes one Marie Single, who in 1947 became the first woman hitcher to circumnavigate that continent. By that time, Claudette Colbert had proved to Clark Gable that the leg was mightier than the thumb, and few young Americans of either sex would have thought twice about flagging a ride if they found themselves short of cash and in need of transportation.

Just how ubiquitous the practice had become is suggested by the opening paragraph of an odd article the hitchhiking historian Bernd Wechner has reprinted from a 1940 edition of the London *Times*:

If any man has hitherto been the symbol of freedom, he is the hitch-hiker. His brother, who travels by rail but without a ticket, has to do so furtively and in fear of penalties. But the hitch-hiker who travels free by road is always above-board. His face and his beseeching thumb are his fortune, and he moves erratically in other people's cars across the great American Continent. It is consequently something of a portent and a warning to learn that even the hitchhiker is now being organized, that there is a College of Hitch-Hikers, and that membership gives the right to the letters R.C.T., which stand for Registered Collegiate Thumber. The advantages are a card of respectability which can be waved before hesitant motorists whose heads are too full of crime stories for them to stop without misgiving. The subscription is a mere half-dollar, and the reward is membership of the (pedestrian) aristocracy of the road.

Wechner adds that he can find no further mention of this ambulant confederation, which hardly seems surprising. If it was successful for a time, it must have served roughly the purpose of the modern-day "ride board," helping college kids who needed to get somewhere cheaply and safely, but it would have been of little use to those who are drawn to the roadside by the love of random encounters and the serendipity of unplanned diversions—that is, anyone likely to become a long-term hitchhiker.

The early 1940s found more occasional hitchers on the road than at any time in American history. Automobiles had become common, but in the war years gas rationing made long trips impossible and discouraged even a lot of ordinary commuters from using their own cars. My father, for example, was working at the Dartmouth Eye Institute in New Hampshire, and hitchhiked to work and back every day—an experience he treasured as his only opportunity to interact on a regular basis with the locals, who were suspicious of "flatlanders" and city folk. Soldiers routinely hitched from their homes to their bases, and from the bases into town when they had a night off or a weekend pass. For a time, hitchhiking became so respectable that Emily Post even provided car-stopping advice for women working in defense plants.

It was also in the forties that the people who would become known as "Beats" did most of their roaming, and over the next decades their poems, novels, music, and larger-than-life personae would inspire a generation to hold up hitchhiking as not merely a mode of transportation but a mythic quest for freedom. The avant-garde composer Harry Partch set an early model with his 1941 oratorio, *Barstow: Eight Hitchhiker Inscriptions from a Highway Railing at Barstow, California*, which opens with the melodious verse, "It's January 26. I'm freezing. Ed Fitzgerald. Age nineteen, five feet ten inches, black hair, brown eyes. Going home to Boston, Massachusetts. It's four, and I'm hungry and broke. . . ."

The Beats were crazy enough in their multifarious ways, but few cared to personify my fellow Bostonian's dismal inscription, and though they are routinely hailed as creators of the hitchhiking mythos, most preferred to stay off the roadside when they had a little cash in their pockets and other means of transportation were available. Gregory Corso's "Poets Hitchhiking on the Highway" hymns a metaphysical duel between two word-mad wanderers, but in general the Beats were drawn to urban streets, mountain retreats, the bustling humanity of bus stations, and the existential solitude of their own cars, racing ever onwards through the American night. Jack Kerouac inspired more hitchhikers than anyone on earth, but it was his legend rather than his writing that got people out on the road—he hitched when he had to, but his roadside tales involve as much grumbling as adventure, and he was happier in a big drive-away with Neal at the wheel. It was movement the Beats loved, whether by bus, train, car, or a mainline shot of heroin—trips to the edge, not polite interchanges with hospitable drivers interspersed with freezing nights in Barstow.

The 1950s brought not only *On the Road*, but also the first serious study of the art—John T. Schlebecker's "An Informal History of Hitchhiking," published in 1958 by *The Historian*—and the first professional hitchhiker, DeVon Smith. A colorful character who would resurface in the twenty-first century as an "outsider artist," creating an extended family of junk-metal robots, Smith received national acclaim in 1957 for hitchhiking the forty-eight continental United States in thirty-three days, and the following year made another celebrated trip, hitching from Neptune, New Jersey, to such exotically named locales as Jupiter, Florida; Pluto, West Virginia; and Earth, Texas, in what he termed "The First Interplanetary Journey on Earth." By 1971, he had hitched a total of 291,000 miles, earning himself a listing in the *Guinness Book of World Records* that would remain unchallenged until the mid-1980s.

Other champion hitchhikers followed Smith's example, but none with his élan, and impressive as their amassed miles may be, it is hard to summon much enthusiasm for their feats. Like the world's fastest portrait painter or all-time marathon violinist, they are curiosities whose pursuit of a purely numeric immortality renders their accomplishments depressingly prosaic. Hitchhiking is, by its nature, an informal and unquantifiable exercise, and watching the clock or counting kilometers runs counter to the spirit of openness and adventure that is its principal attraction. The travelers who best personify hitchhiking's most celebrated era were not the unique and fanatical few, but the anonymous thousands who took to the road, inspired by the Beats, the hippies, the rambling folksingers, or just by the urge to see something beyond familiar streets and faces.

The sixties and seventies were not exactly a golden age of hitchhiking—the crowded entrance ramps, with lines of college students wearily holding their signs, are nostalgic memories only for those who saw them from passing car windows—but they were in one respect unique: for those few years, the roads were full of people who chose to be there, hitching not out of necessity but for pleasure. Today, that thought no doubt strikes many readers as bizarre, or even as a perverse affectation, as if we were choosing to crawl or panhandle for fun. But for some twenty years, it was part of the common culture. Paul Simon wrote of hitchhiking off "to look for America," and even after they became stars, his partner Art Garfunkel sometimes rejected chartered plane flights and thumbed his way to gigs.

It was not just an American phenomenon, either. Young people were hitchhiking across Asia, Africa, South America, Oceania, and to every corner of Europe. Guidebooks routinely included hitching tips, and Harvard University's *Let's Go* series made its cover logo a hand with an extended thumb. Then, sometime in the 1980s, the freeze set in. It didn't happen all at once, but as I wandered I saw fewer and fewer people on the roads, and heard more and more warnings. Articles began to appear about "the death of hitchhiking," and later, nostalgic pieces about the good old days when hitching was still possible.

But this is not a book about the past, nor am I vying for the title of "world's last hitchhiker." The roads no longer teem with cheerful optimists, but we are not by any means a dying breed. There are several dozen hitchhiking Internet sites, and they reveal an active subculture of young thumbers. Perusing the biographies of current pop stars, one still finds claims of hitchhiking experience—most often, oddly, by women: Michelle Shocked, Ani DiFranco, Courtney Love, and Jewel all tell road stories—and for the same reasons it attracted their predecessors. It is cheap, and easy, and exciting, and it puts you in touch with the world around you as no other form of travel can. So consider this chapter just one more ride; there will be other writers to pick up the history where I leave it.

THE ART AND SCIENCE

OF HITCHHIKING

As noted by The Hiker and the *Herald* correspondent, by the 1920s there were already seasoned adepts who viewed hitchhiking as an art or science. Some readers will think this attitude absurd, since those who have only viewed us at a distance or hitched once or twice will not have considered the technical intricacies of the task. You just stick out your thumb, and wait for someone to stop—what could be more obvious? And yet, the longer one spends on the road, the more appreciation one gains for the skills involved.

I suppose it is the same with anything that people do long enough. To keep your sense of pride or sense of self alive, you try to do it well. So most longtime hitchers develop rules and methodologies, and tend to be as boring and disputatious about them as masters of any arcane craft. We fancy ourselves psychologists of traffic, having spent innumerable hours on the roadside working out why one driver stops and others pass on by. Admittedly, when viewed with the cold eye of the more rigorous sciences, our experimental methodology leaves much to be desired. The problem is that while a driver sometimes will tell us why he or she chose to stop, we are never told why all the others continued blithely past. And even on a good day, the cars that pass outnumber the ones that stop, usually by a hundred or more to one. All dedicated hitchhikers must thus be of a disposition to judge the proverbial glass half full—or more accurately, to be encouraged just by knowing that there is a little water out there somewhere. You cannot afford to dwell on the proportion of stoppers to passers, because that way lies despair. You just note the Good Samaritans, and let the other drivers drift by like inchoate ghosts.

Or rather, you forget the ones that didn't stop once they have passed you by. Until then, they are all potential rides. And that is where the technique comes in, because drivers as a class cannot be separated into those who do and those who don't stop. Whether a particular driver stops or drives by on any particular day is in the vast majority of cases a matter of momentary chance rather than of fixed principle or character. There are a saintly few who always stop, and an admittedly far greater number who never do—or, more accurately and optimistically, who never have—but most can be persuaded to take a rider when in the right mood and approached in the right manner, or to bypass someone who rubs them somehow wrong.

The technical questions of hitchhiking can be divided into three basic categories: who, where, and how. Addressing the most obvious of these, let's start with where: Dilettante hitchers often place themselves on blind curves or at spots where there is no place to pull over. Thanks to the basic decency of humankind, they eventually get rides, but they do not impress observers with their intelligence or empathy. The basic rule in choosing a spot is to select one where you can be seen as far off as possible and there is plenty of room for even the most cautious driver to stop. On a slow road through a small town, a driveway may be enough, but if you hope for a semi to pull over on the interstate, a hundred yards of breakdown lane is a none-too-elegant sufficiency.

There are also some larger geographical issues: It is almost always hard to leave a major city, and the difficulties of this task have been exacerbated by the construction of limited-access highways. On traditional roads, you simply walk or take a bus out to the edge of town, find a promising-looking spot, and stick out your thumb, but there are no good spots on downtown urban entrance ramps. The result is that you have to do some research, and the usual tourist-information sources are ill-equipped to give hitchhiking advice. Often, the only option is to inspect a map, select a random entrance ramp that looks as if it will be in a rural enough setting to provide a breakdown lane where cars can stop for you, then make your way out to it by bus and foot, and hope that luck is on your side. A variation on this arises if the map shows a highway rest stop or restaurant within a few hundred yards of the ramp, in which case you may be able to walk along the shoulder to this oasis, hoping that the cops don't pass and throw you off en route. Or you can start out along an alternate road, where it is legal to hitch, and intersect the highway at some point outside of town—though this will often leave you frustrated for hours, watching local traffic crawling past, none of the drivers interested in your plight or likely to substantially relieve it even if they stopped for you. Or then again, you can try to find a friend or helpful trucker who will drive you out onto the highway, and drop you at the first rest area—the method I employed to exit Boston at the commencement of this trip.

Even if you find the perfect spot, leaving a major city is often a slow business—just as it is relatively easy to get a ride into one once you are within its geographical orbit. Partly, this is a matter of capillaries versus arteries: there are many exits from a city, and any one of them carries only a fraction of the outbound traffic, while going in you catch the cars before they branch off the main stream. Also, most cars heading out of a city are going only to the suburbs, and for those going further, the temptation to stop in heavy urban traffic is less than on a clear road—and here we are beginning to get into the realm of psychology rather than geographical placement.

A driver starting out on a trip is not yet bored and eager for companionship, or caught up in the rhythm of travel and ready to welcome a roadside wanderer as a kindred spirit. And the question of shared goals has its more prosaic side as well: The cars leaving Boston on the Massachusetts Turnpike may be bound for anyplace from Worcester to Washington, Alaska, or Acapulco. Drivers setting off on a long journey are often reluctant to stop for someone who could grow into an annoyance over hours or days of travel. Contrariwise, if they are going only a few miles up the road, they may think you would not want such piddling assistance.

You also tend to get rides more quickly if the drivers think they know where you are going. Heading toward a big city, everyone assumes you are going there, and when they share your destination they are more likely to pick you up. Heading away, you might be going anywhere, and many drivers will use that as an excuse to pass you by, preferring not to waste time on a roadside colloquy that could reveal nonintersecting travel plans. (Of course, you can use a sign, but let us postpone that discussion for a moment.)

Once out on the road, matters are a good deal simpler. You have a ride, and it will leave you either where you want to stop or where the driver has to turn off. Again, the limited-access highways present their special problems: some entrance ramps are ideal for hitching, while others are adorned with faded inscriptions left by previous visitors who have been stuck for days, and it is not always obvious which are of which variety. You can avoid this dilemma by always getting out at rest stops, and if the weather is dicey or speed is an issue, this is the way to go. But sometimes your driver is not going to pass a rest stop; maybe you grabbed a lift just to get you across a state line, or maybe your driver decides to make an unexpected detour. In that case, you just have to check your map, ask advice, and hope for the best.

On traditional roads, you move more slowly, but you also are in closer touch with the countryside. You get more rides from locals, and have more choices, as every side road is an option to be weighed. And if the weather is pleasant you can walk, rather than having to stand in one spot watching other people go their way. Out in the middle of the United States, though, you always run the risk of getting stranded, beyond walking distance from anyplace where you could find even a drink of water. The distances are vast, and there is no feeling quite like seeing your erstwhile host turn off on a little road that disappears through fields stretching to the horizon, and realizing that you have barely seen another car in the last thirty miles and shortly it will be dark. That said, on quiet, lazy days, the smaller country roads provide some of hitchhiking's most pleasant moments. As short ride follows short ride, you take a rolling poll of the populace, and there are no bad hitching spots, since folks can stop right on the road and chat a while, with no fear of annoying their equally relaxed neighbors.

But back to the art and science. To formulate the "where" rules compactly: be where the drivers can see you, where they have a place to stop, and where they will think you are headed the same way they are. Of course, one cannot always find a spot that fulfills all three requirements, but that is a good basic guideline.

The "who" of hitchhiking is rarely considered, but obviously a key question. Go out on the road looking like a grunge rocker, with an aggressive T-shirt and multiple piercings, and you will have exactly the effect you might expect: other grunge-rock fans will be more tempted to pick you up, while people who hate grungy rockers will stamp on the gas pedal. Likewise with those who choose to hitchhike in suits or cowboy outfits. Basically, people tend to pick up riders who look like the sort of people they hang out with in other situations, or like romantic figures they have always wanted to meet. Hence the advantage of not wearing too obvious a cultural uniform, and of having a guitar slung over your shoulder. It is important to look clean and unthreatening, but it also helps to look as if you belong on the road. I have had drivers tell me that they only pick up backpackers or people who look like students—that is, they don't want bums in their car, but are happy to help out young vacationers. In a lot of countries (as at one time in the United States) it is common for soldiers to hitch to and from army bases in uniform, for exactly this reason: drivers instantly know who they are and why they are out there, and consider them a different class from transient civilians. This is also why it helps to have a guitar clearly visible. Drivers often tell me that they picked me up because of it, and while they may like music or play guitar themselves, what is most important is that I fit their image of who a hitchhiker should be. The wandering minstrel is a storybook staple, so people accept me as belonging on the highway, pursuing my profession—not very successfully, perhaps, but in time-honored fashion.

This brings us to the "how" of hitching, which adds further layers, vaguer and more subject to argument—because anyone can carry a guitar as bait for rides, whether or not they play the instrument, and thus take advantage of the minstrel image. I have never heard of anyone doing exactly that, but other gimmicks have entered the common lore of the craft. I have several times been told of hitchhikers who packed their clothes in a modified plastic gasoline can, creating the illusion that they were stranded motorists. I have never actually met one of these savvy travelers, and they may be nothing more than roadside mythology—besides which, I am a bit dubious about the efficacy of the ruse: I would expect it to attract drivers who were just headed to the next turnoff, and many of them would resent the subterfuge. But then again, those drawbacks might be balanced by the number of drivers who were persuaded to stop. In any case, one is not always on the roadside, and a gas can is hardly the most comfortable or efficient piece of luggage for a long journey. It is tempting to try it, though, if only for experimental purposes.

I once met a hitchhiker who packed all his belongings in a black leather briefcase. He was clean-cut and looked thoroughly respectable and unadventurous, possibly a businessman who had missed his train and needed to get to an important meeting. The beauty of this guise was that it was as useful off the road as on. It even took care of his sleeping requirements: when stranded in a strange city, he could walk unchallenged into an office building, take the elevator to the top floor, find a quiet spot, and sleep there, with his respectable overcoat as bedding.

Of course, different drivers are attracted to different looks. A truck driver may turn a blind eye to guitarists, backpackers, and stranded businessmen, and yet be happy to offer a ride to someone who looks as if he is out of work, down on his luck, but last month might have been driving a truck. Your workingman hitchhiker can sometimes be seen on the side of a highway, especially in the prairie states, but much of the time he just walks into truck stops and asks around for a ride headed his way. This is a good technique in any case, but ideal for someone who looks more like a trucker than a college student. There is also the matter of pride: a lot of people, even if they are out of money—sometimes especially when they are out of money—don't want to seem to be begging, so they would rather strike up a casual conversation that might lead to the offer of a ride than stand by the highway with their thumb in the air.

This direct approach is one of the lesser-known standbys of the hitchhiking repertoire. When people say that nobody hitchhikes anymore, or that it is much harder for dark-skinned travelers to get rides, or that there is no way a woman can safely do it, they are ignoring this option. It is perfectly possible to hitchhike from coast to coast without ever flagging down a moving car. Waiting on a rest area or at a truck stop, you can pick your drivers, walk up to them, and work everything out in a situation where you can size each other up. There are drivers of both genders and many ethnicities, if you want to be particular. And even if you are embarrassed or don't much care for the direct approach, it can become the only option in some circumstances. At night, very few people will pull over on the open highway, but plenty are eager to have a companion to help keep them awake, if they first meet you face-to-face in a well-lighted environment. So before assuming that no one hitchhikes, remember that we need not be standing out where we are visible. Who knows how many free riders are still flitting back and forth across the country, but never surfacing to be counted? I have even heard of hitchhikers who traveled with their own CB radios to call trucks off the highway—to me, a bulky and overly technological solution, robbing the enterprise of its romance and cutting down unnecessarily on the range of transport, but no doubt quite effective.

But suppose you prefer to stand on the road, in plain sight, tempting the fates. There remains the most contentious question of hitchhiking technique: to use a sign or not to use a sign. There is no subject more disputed among longtime hitchhikers. Some feel that it is idiocy to be out there without something to indicate your destination, while others consider signs a waste of time, a cheat, and a distraction. There are places where the former have a very strong case, as when you are stuck on an entrance ramp to a highway that will shortly split. In that situation, a simple placard reading "West" can make all the difference, tempting the drivers who are headed that way and preventing futile delays and annoyance for those who happen to be going east. A sign can also be a definite aid if you are on a major road but only want to go a short distance. For example, if you are headed into Iowa City and get dropped off ten miles away on I-80, a sign is invaluable, since drivers who are stopping only ten miles on will assume that a hitcher on the interstate is going further, while the drivers who are going further will tend to take you only as far as the exit ramp, leaving you with a long walk into town.

I always carry a black marker suitable for sign writing, but use it only for such special occasions. The great advantage of a sign, aside from making you look prepared and efficient, is that it lets the drivers know where you are going, and most of the time I don't want the drivers to associate me with a precise destination, since that will scare off the ones who are not going there. This would obviously be true if I were outside Boston with a sign saying "Chicago," and the driver was headed south to New York City, but it seems to be a quirk of psychology that the Chicago sign would even discourage a lot of drivers who were headed for places like Albany or Rochester, several hundred miles along my chosen path. After all, they are not going to Chicago, and my sign says I want a ride to Chicago, and many drivers read signs literally. The same problem pertains if you try to write out your destinations incrementally: a sign that says "Albany" will provide an excuse for some Chicago-bound drivers to pass you by. (Or maybe not. As previously noted, you never really know the motivations of the ones who didn't stop. Like most hitchhikers' wisdom, this is half-informed musing, developed over years of watching unstopped cars pass me by, but unverifiable.) Many longtime hitchers swear by directional signage, and avoid these pitfalls by simply carrying a sign saying "West" all the way across the country. And some sign bearers eschew directional indicators entirely, considering their sign more a courtesy and costume than a source of precise information. I knew an English lad who carried a sign that simply said:

PLEASE!

Eighteen years old, with the well-scrubbed look of a schoolboy on holiday, he made a singularly inoffensive spectacle, and undoubtedly excited the parental sympathies of many motorists. To those whose hearts were not softened, however, he shortly revealed another facet of his personality: The back of his sign was printed—in reversed lettering, to be read in rear-view mirrors—with the message:

!ʍƎHT ℲℲO ʞↃ∩Ⅎ

For a few years, I joined the ranks of the sign carriers. My conversion experience came one day in the early 1980s, when I was stuck on a hot, dry highway in the middle of South Dakota, and all the drivers kept signaling that they were turning off or stopping up the road. I was tired and thirsty, and would have been happy just to get a lift to a convenience store or a gas station, or anywhere with running water. Besides which, I had been standing out there for three hours, and even if it didn't materially improve my condition, I wanted to have my faith in humanity restored and be reminded that I would not spend the rest of my life in that spot. So eventually I hunted up a discarded cardboard box, cut off a suitable section, and made a sign that said, No Ride Is Too Short. It worked, and when I found myself in a similar situation a few days later I tried it again and it worked that time as well. Further experimentation established the odd fact that this sign not only served its original purpose—stopping drivers who were only going short distances—but was equally effective with long-range travelers. Indeed, it proved its worth most decisively on a trip across Canada, when it rescued me from that once-common hitchhikers' nightmare, the overpopulated entrance ramp. I had been dropped at an intersection with the Trans-Canada Highway outside Calgary, where the northern road came down from Edmonton, right after the Edmonton Folk Festival. I don't know if it was the festival crowd or just normal Canadian summer conditions, but as I walked down the ramp and onto the eastbound breakdown lane, I passed more than two dozen other hitchhikers, in varying stages of dustiness and frustration. There were single men, couples, pairs of women, many of them looking proper, safe, and student-like, and all obviously inured to a long, long wait. With fatalistic determination, I plodded to the end of the queue, which was spaced out for a good half-mile. I put down my pack, held up my sign, and a car sped past, slammed on its brakes, roared back, and picked me up. The driver was an amateur stock car racer from South Carolina, his tape player loaded with beach music and the complete works of Jimmy Buffett, and he was going all the way to Montreal. "I couldn't pass up that sign," he said, and we were off on the fastest ride of my life. Despite the fact that much of the highway was winding, two-lane road, he averaged eighty miles per hour including stops for meals, and his driving was absolutely magical: He never screeched around a turn or passed when he didn't have proper visibility, it all felt smooth and easy, and we were in Montreal in two days.

And yet, a sign is one more thing to carry. Granted, it is a minimal burden, but why be burdened at all when a naked thumb is sufficient to the task at hand? Besides which, if you're holding a sign, you can't play guitar. So these days I keep a slab of white cardboard strapped to the front of my pack, but there it remains until I find myself in a predicament that calls for more explicit and precise communication than I can manage with a thumb and a wide smile.

I suppose that if we define our terms a bit more broadly, that smile itself might be considered a sort of sign. It has nothing to do with my mood, after all. It is a purely functional expression that spreads itself automatically across my face, utterly detached from any thought or emotion, and is meant to convey the vital information that I am a cheerful, harmless fellow. I may be cold and wet, stranded for hours and cursing every passing vehicle, but it endures, placid and unaffected as the gold leaf on a baroque cherub. When seen up close, it is actually rather ridiculous. It is a stage smile, intended to be viewed from a distance, and like a stage actor's gestures is somewhat grotesque when taken out of context. What is more, its production is entirely unconscious: If I put out my thumb, the smile appears. The connection might as well be mechanical, a system of tendons running directly from my right hand—or my left hand in Britain and some Commonwealth countries—to my facial muscles. But it serves its purpose. Once, on the northern coast of Scotland, an elderly couple picked me up, and the wife explained that they had passed me by because they were just going a little way up the road and never stopped for people, but she could not get my smile out of her mind and finally told her husband to turn around and go back.

Is there something disturbing about this empty simulacrum of good cheer? Call me a faker if you will, but we all have our automatic smiles, our mechanical sounds of encouragement, our little, ingrained habits designed to make others think better of us. Etiquette is not a bad thing. It makes everyone's life easier, oiling the gears of all our social interactions. Nor is my facial gilding an inexorably thin and meaningless veneer. As counterfeit as that smile may be out on the roadside, it mutates into good, solid coin as soon as anyone has the courtesy to stop and give me a lift. No matter how long the wait, nothing shifts faster than the mood of a stranded hitchhiker when a car pulls over and your faith in humanity is once again rewarded.

Which brings up one last category of road technique: the proper behavior once you have a ride. If you want a long lift, you have to be a pleasant companion, and even if you are riding just a few miles you want the driver to feel good about the experience, so he or she will be encouraged to pull over in the future.

One excellent maxim for hitchhiking comportment is "speak when spoken to." Most drivers want to talk, but some do not, and when one is cruising down the highway in placid contemplation of the universe and stops from simple charity, there is nothing more annoying than an insistently chatty hitchhiker. So once you have expressed your gratitude and made sure the ride is headed in the right direction, keep quiet and let the driver set the mood. Usually, he or she will break the silence right away, asking where you're coming from and where you're going, then moving on to other subjects. When drivers stop, it is usually because they welcome company, and as a rule they will be happiest if they do most of the talking themselves. They have done you a favor by picking you up, and you can return it by nodding appreciatively and making encouraging remarks at suitable intervals as they direct the conversation.

Even if the driver is quiet at first, you should remain potentially attentive. Non-hitchers have sometimes asked me if I carry a book or a headset to alleviate the boredom on long rides, not understanding that it is the rider's job to be companionable. The driver can turn up the radio and ignore you, but you should be ready anytime she decides to turn it down and begin a conversation. It is her car, after all, and you are a guest. She can smoke or play loud music, and if it bothers you, your only polite recourse is to get out at the next convenient stopping place.

Another question that non-hitchers sometimes ask is what I do if I need to go to the bathroom and my driver shows no sign of stopping anytime soon. My answer, though I know it is unsatisfactory, is that in my experience drivers are as human as riders, and stop often enough that the issue doesn't arise. Good etiquette, especially with truckers on tight schedules, is to try to match them mile for mile and hour for hour, so, as with long bus trips in third world countries, you just put your body into a state of suspended animation—though obviously, the time may come when you have to speak up.

A more tricky problem, for me at least, is how to stay awake. Especially on warm days, on quiet roads, I have a tendency to drowse off when the conversation lags, and to this day I haven't found a trick that would keep me consistently alert. Most drivers have been understanding, but it is an embarrassing situation, and a few have clearly been annoyed. Especially at night, a lot of drivers pick you up to keep themselves awake, and the last thing they want is to have you snoring in the passenger seat—a disinclination with which any safety-conscious rider will be quick to sympathize. At times, I have broken my first rule and forced a conversation simply to keep from drifting off. At others, I must admit, I have given in and slept, but in general if I'm that tired I try to get off the road until I've had some rest.

And now, one final item cannot be avoided: rarely, but inevitably, if you hitchhike long enough you will find yourself in a situation where you want to get the hell out. As I've already remarked, I have never been assaulted or even threatened by a driver, but have had several who were drunk, a few who were weird or crazy, and a handful who picked me up in hopes of messing with my tender flesh. When possible, of course, you should avoid such situations. If a driver pulls over and something about him strikes you wrong, the best move is to make your excuses and stay out of the car, even though you may have been waiting for hours in the pouring rain. And that advice goes double if the car has other people in it, and triple if you are a woman and the other people are all men. If you get caught, though, you just have to keep your head, do whatever you can to defuse the situation, and get out as soon as you can. If you have the slightest doubt about a driver, you should keep your luggage within easy reach and make sure you know how to work the door handle. And that is really all that can be said, except that life is always a gamble, whether we want it to be or not, so all you can do is hope that the rewards outweigh the dangers—and remember that the more experience you have, the better off you will be when things get tough.

A VEHICULAR TAXONOMY, OR NATURAL HISTORY OF THE HIGHWAY

The time is coming when we should get back on the road. However, before we end our examination of hitching as an art and science, it seems appropriate to take a moment to consider the range of conveyances most commonly encountered. Without recapitulating an exhaustive list of motor vehicles, one may yet set down a catalog of their attributes as particularly related to the hitchhiker's interests, with the advantages and disadvantages of each. Taxonomy, after all, is to a great extent relative. Gorillas and human beings belong to the same branch of the primate family, descended from a common ancestor who remained in Africa while the grandparents of modern-day orangutans split off and wandered east—and yet we file orangutans and gorillas in one category, calling them apes, while filing ourselves separately. This contradicts the supposedly immutable logic of genetics, but is in perfect keeping with the broader scientific enterprise, which at root is simply an extended exercise in separating ourselves from our erstwhile cousins in the animal kingdom. In the same way, Americans routinely and unconsciously divide people by race according to our own local norms: in Boston, I am considered white although my grandparents were all Jewish, but when I spoke of myself as white in Mississippi a young African-American woman suggested I must be "some kind of mix," and, informed of my Jewishness, responded, "Hell, I thought so. That ain't white." Such taxonomies are the common currency of our lives, though we rarely note them. If we need to pound a nail and do not have our toolbox handy, any solid object can be reclassified as a hammer.

The Kalam people of New Guinea, though perfectly aware that birds have feathers, frogs are smooth-skinned, and mammals are furry, group them all into three broad categories based on their usefulness as food: *kmn* for large animals, *as* for smaller ones, and *kopyak* for rats. Hitchhikers take a similar view of the varieties of passing traffic: what matters is not whether a passing vehicle is a Ford or a Volvo, but whether it is likely to stop and what sort of ride it will provide if it does. I am even tempted to adapt the precise Kalam categories to describe highway traffic, since from the hitchhiker's point of view there is a similarly tripartite division: our kmn are the trucks, which not only carry us, but introduce us into an aristocracy of the road; our as provide transportation only, welcome though it may be; while our kopyak would be motorcycles, tractors, and bicycles, which simply clutter up the road without being any use to us.

However, in honor of previous scholarship, I will instead adopt the taxonomy of the book trade, and categorize the denizens of the highway as if they were volumes of print—and that too has its peculiar aptness, for in their way all drivers serve a traveler as so many volumes of information or entertainment, opening themselves to us and giving us another person's picture of the world. What else does any book do? They are all brief visits with other people, providing company for as long as their matter carries us along, then leaving us to pull another volume from the shelf.

Thus, for the highway as for the library, let us group our choices by size and shape, into folio, quarto, octavo, and duodecimo.

Folio I

Among the folio conveyances, the most common and coveted is the semi, or tractor-trailer. These are of various genera, including Macks, Freightliners, Peterbilts, Kenworths, and Volvos, though to the hitchhiker the differences between them are generally not worth noting. All are excellent rides, their only disadvantage being that in some areas they are hobbled by lower speed limits than pertain for smaller traffic, and that when overloaded they can be very slow getting up mountains (as well as hard to brake coming down the other side—but that is a matter to be banished from our minds whenever possible). The semi is made up of two distinct sections: the tractor, which provides the motive power and contains the brain and living quarters of the vehicle, and the trailer, which hitchhikers generally consider to be an appendage as irrelevant as their vestigial appendix, albeit far larger. I have only once ridden in the trailer section of a semi. That was in Spain, where I was picked up by a truck hauling five elephants to a circus in Madrid. The drivers, who were also the elephants' trainers, said that they had no extra room in the cab, but that I was welcome to ride in the front section of the trailer, where they kept the hay. The only disadvantages to this were 1) that I would be locked in, and there was no window, nor any way to communicate with my hosts, and 2) that the two most forward elephants were accustomed to reaching their trunks over the barrier between the front and back compartments and stealing hay. Who could resist a ride like that? Two days, locked in the back of a truck, bleary with hay fever, punching elephants in the trunk and yelling for them to behave. It remains a treasured memory. In general, though, one rides up front.

For highway travel, there is no more pleasant place to ride than in a semi cab. They have plenty of leg room, lots of space for luggage, and the seats are designed for long-haul riders. Their windows, spacious and high above the ground, afford unparalleled vistas for the lover of scenery. There is also a section in the rear of the cab equipped for sleeping, generally with a single bed but sometimes with a second, upper bunk that folds against the wall when not in use. Truckers driving solo often use this upper bed as storage space, but occasionally have been known to clear it and offer it to a long-distance guest.

Along with the comforts of the cab, the semi provides a welcome degree of safety, being relatively impervious to the adversities both of nature and of amateur motorists. One occasionally sees the carcass of an eighteen-wheeler upset on the roadside, its belly spewing ruined merchandise, but generally when truck and car collide, the trucker walks away unscathed. (I once had the pleasure of driving a Citroën 2CV into an oncoming truck outside Amritsar, India. The Citroën crumpled like a beer can on a frat brother's forehead—fortunately absorbing much of the impact of the collision—while the truck was hardly scratched.) The size, weight, and durability of the vehicles are complemented by the professional expertise of the operators. Granted, one finds truckers who are reckless, insane, wired, or in the grips of complete mental and physical exhaustion, but in general they are expert, reliable, and familiar with the curves and contours of the road ahead, as well as with the meteorological vicissitudes of each region.

Along with the corporeal comforts of the great trucks, there are also the spiritual advantages that accrue when traveling in their sphere. I have discussed the bathing facilities and separate dining arrangements that truckers enjoy, and these are part of a larger picture. Truckers live on the highways, and are as much in their element there as whales are in the ocean. They have their own systems of communication, and receive constant bulletins about what is up the road. More than that, they are always among comrades, and there is a relaxation in their relationship to travel. Or maybe the point is that for them it is not travel. The great in-between is where they live, as sailors live on the sea, and it is the periods in port that relieve the monotony and provide the sort of vacation and variety that settled people derive from motion. In that sense, riding with truckers is not simply a way of covering miles or getting from one town to another, but a visit to a foreign place and an exotic society, with its own rules and customs.

Not all of those customs are to my taste, nor would I want to live the trucking life, any more than I would care to move to an Inuit village or a South Sea island. I love riding in trucks, but there are disadvantages as well—though I can easily forget them as I roll warm and cozy through the darkness of the Great Plains. There is the noise, for one thing, which in the older cabs can be overwhelming, and this is exacerbated by the crackle of the CB, a spiky background of static interrupted by queries about cops and scales and predictable comments on blondes in convertibles. A lot of truckers find the CB chatter reassuring and companionable, an electronic counterpart to the old-time sailor's similarly repetitious parrot, but to a visitor it can be as distracting as a television set in an otherwise pleasant bar.

There is also the unrelenting momentum of the trucking life. As a hitchhiker, you are free to stop at any time, but that is easy to forget when you are caught up in the long-haul orbit: coast to coast in three days, pausing every five or six hours for a bathroom break and a bite, then off again, rolling through the sun and rain, morning, noon, and night, passing towns that will forever be only names on signs even if passed a thousand times. There is a hypnotic lure to this world, but after a while it can begin to feel like a trap, and make you yearn to jump off and grab some little rides with sightseers and traveling salesmen.

Folio II

The semis are the unchallenged mammoths of the highways, but they are not alone in the folio category. There are buses, for example. Admittedly, in the annals of long-haul travel, the bus rates low in terms of comfort and romance. *It Happened One Night* notwithstanding, there is little bus-riding legend or lore, nor do I intend to add much to this meager store. And yet, it must be noted that the bus as a species is too often ignored by hitchhikers. How many of us have retracted our thumbs, or turned our usual hand-stance to a wave, assuming them unhitchable? But buses do stop. Not often, but that only increases the thrill when it happens. Once, in Idaho, I had a lift from a man who had remodeled a school bus into his home and traveling sculpture studio. An East Coast expatriate, with a bushy beard and battered felt hat, he carried me for an hour or so, providing both scintillating conversation and an unprecedented amount of leg room. In Mexico, I once got a ride in a bus carrying a baseball team to an out-of-town game. Leaving Boston for New York, I was picked up by a Green Tortoise bus en route to California with a dozen fare-paying passengers—a couple grumbled at my getting a free ride, but the rest were glad to have a guitarist aboard and we staged a small rolling hootenanny. And there was an afternoon in Sinaloa, Mexico, when I had been waiting an hour on the dry, hot road to Culiacan. A public bus pulled up, and I figured, what the hell, I might as well pay a few bucks and get to a better place. I mounted the steps, reaching for my wallet, and the conductor said, "No, no, we saw you hitchhiking, it's OK." The front passengers smiled at me in a curious, friendly way: I was an unexpected but quite welcome novelty. So, while I would not rely on buses, I always hitch them on the off-chance. Especially the band buses. I've never heard of Merle or Willie telling his driver to pull over for a roadside guitarist, but it would be nice to be the first.

Quarto I

Arriving at the Quarto rides, we find a motley assortment that includes campers, SUVs, pickup trucks, moving vans, ambulances, minibuses, and various sorts of local work vehicles—cement mixers, dump trucks, and suchlike. Of these, the one most frequently of service is the pickup. Pickup rides are common in rural areas, as are the vehicles themselves, and they are not typically long-haul, though there are exceptions to that rule. In any case, what is unique about the pickup is that its hospitality comes in two quite distinct forms: inside and outside.

Depending on the driver, the front of a pickup can feel like the front seat of an ordinary car or the cab of a small truck. In the former case, it is a perfectly nice ride but nothing special, while in the latter it lacks the comfort or elevation of a semi cab, and can be rather cramped, especially if there are more than two people in it or, as frequently happens, it is crammed with tool boxes or other work-related objects.

The back of a pickup is a very different matter. I have ridden in pickup beds all over the world, and in a multifarious array of circumstances. Some were functioning as country buses, some were private vehicles that happened to be full-up in front but had space in the rear (often shared with children or dogs), some were driven by women who did not trust a strange man to join them in the cab but had no misgivings about hauling one in back.

In fine weather and open country, these can be the pleasantest of rides. The breeze keeps you fresh and alert, and you are outside with all the smells and sights, your experience undiluted by windows and artificial climate controls. For the meditative traveler, there is also the advantage that one is not called upon to be sociable. Like a train-hopper, you are riding back where the freight travels, while the drivers are up front in upholstered, windowed comfort—though in this case they will sometimes roll down or slide open a window and pass you a can of beer, which provides a nice change. The drawback of these rides is that their comforts can shift quite literally with the wind. The most pleasurable pickup bed becomes a good deal less so with a chill breeze, and far less so with a shower of rain—though in some circumstances even a cold, wet ride is better than nothing.

One final feature of the pickup ride that must be considered is its legal standing: In some states, drivers are prohibited from carrying passengers in the truck bed, and I once had to ride from Grass Valley, California, to downtown Oakland lying on my back and seeing nothing but clouds and an occasional bird, so as not to be visible to passing highway patrolmen. It was pleasant enough as a novelty, but not an experience I would want to repeat with any frequency.

Quarto II

Though pickups provide the most common rides of the quarto variety, that is not because they are the most common vehicles of this class on the roads. These days, SUVs vastly outnumber them on most highways—a subject to be pursued anon—and on some stretches, at some times of year, so also do RVs, campers, and mobile homes. However, while these vehicles are luxuriously equipped to welcome guests, their promise tends to be as illusory as the mirages that appear to thirsty pilgrims in the desert. In several decades of hitching, only a half-dozen RVs have taken me aboard, and all but two of those were approached directly while stopped, rather than pulled off the road. I have concluded that in a great part this is because an RV is as much a home as a vehicle, and hence inspires a greater sense of both privacy and its flip side, vulnerability—especially considering the advanced age of most inhabitants. If you have a chance to befriend the denizens of a camper in repose, however, engaging them in conversation and allowing them to consider you as a potential houseguest rather than simply a roadside tramp, they can prove exceedingly hospitable, providing not only conveyance but also food, drink, and even overnight accommodations. Unfortunately, for the touristically inclined, their windows are generally small and ill-placed, the better to leave room for cupboards and other homely accoutrements. I have had a couple of exceptional rides in RVs, including one with a French family of four who picked me up on the road outside Ankara, Turkey, paused a day in Istanbul, then continued with not only me but my erstwhile traveling partner all the way to Chambery, in the French Alps, pausing on the way for a lunchtime visit to Venice. They then put us up in their house for several days, and loaned us a car in which we took day-trips around the region. Ever since, I have optimistically hitched all RVs, aware that despite the almost inevitable disappointment, there are amazing possibilities hidden behind those aluminum-sided doors.

Quarto III

The minibus or van falls somewhere between the pickup and the RV. As a work vehicle, it is like the pickup, with the difference that its rear affords no romantic, airy freedom, and in fact is often cramped and dark. There are few rides less memorable than those I have spent sitting on a box in the back of a van, unable to get even a glimpse of passing scenery through the small, dirty windows.

There is of course the minibus of legend, the fabled "hippie van" of the sixties and seventies. In those years, you would automatically heave a sigh of relief as, after hours on an unfriendly stretch of country road, you saw a battered, hand-painted VW appear in the distance, its hirsute driver smiling in friendly complicity as he welcomed you aboard. In Europe, especially, I partook often of that freak community, welcomed as part of the tribe of Kerouac, Kesey, Dylan, and the Grateful Dead—the ride often included an offer of illicit smokables—and occasionally ended up spending a couple of days on a farm or in a big communal house in a college town. I only caught the waning years of that post-beatnik camaraderie, however, and in America have found its promise often frustrated. The most disheartening day I ever spent on the road was my first trip through California, limping down the Pacific Coast Highway from Monterey to Los Angeles. Hippie vans abounded, their sides a gallery of psychedelic paintwork, their drivers shaggy and beaded, their bumper stickers blazoning the virtues of anarchy and organic farming. And they swept past, hour after hour. Eventually, some conservative retiree would pull over, on his way home from a fishing trip, and give me a ride. Then I would watch another three hours of the counterculture roll by, until a Mercedes would stop, driven by a middle-aged middle manager, in a hurry but moved by my obviously desolate circumstances. Then I would be back on the road again, the flower-bedecked vans mocking me with their irrational refusal to conform to cherished stereotype.

Today, even those last benighted vestiges of the Aquarian Age have all but disappeared. The rebel van of the new millennium is more likely emblazoned with a lushly airbrushed western scene or spectral Harley, and offers no suggestion of friendly camaraderie. The communal youth culture has been replaced by rebel individualists, equally uniform in fashions, cliques, and clubbishness, but displaying a leather-jacketed "fuck you" in place of a tie-dyed, patchouli-scented welcome.

Quarto IV

Which brings us to the SUV. Large and comfortable, supersized private cars, one might expect that these would stop as often as coupes or station wagons. Given that they are relatively new to the highways and my recent experience is not as great as the reader might wish, this may even be the case. But none has ever stopped for me. Not once. Happenstance, perhaps, but I suspect a quirk of psychology, an untraced allele that makes the buying of an SUV a marker for a lack of highway hospitality. "I bought it because it's safer" may inextricably go hand in hand with "It's not safe to pick people up," and "I know it's an ecological horror, but I like my comfort" would fit neatly with "I don't think people should travel if they can't pay their way." In any case, the sight of a shiny new Suburban or Explorer cresting the ridge, its lone driver sumptuously supplied with unused passenger space, quickly ceases to excite a surge of optimism in the stranded traveler's heart.

Which is not to say that you shouldn't give them a try. There is nothing to be gained in mistaking pessimism for intelligence, and acting on the assumption that a car is not worth hitching will not increase your chances of getting a ride. Likewise, all the quarto-sized work vehicles rarely stop, but I would not advise anyone to ignore them. I have had rides in rented U-hauls and an electric company repair truck, and had one friend who flagged down an ambulance that took him from Lyons to the south of France, whence it had recently transferred a wealthy invalid to Paris. These rides are rarely outstanding for either speed or comfort, but they are welcome as curiosities and as proof that one never knows what may rise to the lure of a questing and friendly thumb.

Octavo

Of the Octavo vehicles, little need be said. All of my readers will be familiar with the general run of private cars, and all their concomitant comforts. One detail, though, may be worth mentioning, which is that, within some rather elastic limits, cars hold as many people as the driver is willing to carry. My father did not hesitate to stop for hitchhiking couples, although we were already a family of four, and I have had many rides that involved some rearranging of baggage and passengers. These rides have in some cases been excruciatingly uncomfortable in purely physical terms, but were nonetheless welcome for the degree of hospitality displayed. They are particularly cheering, at least to me, when the car is crowded with a family. The children are learning a valuable lesson about the importance of charity and the basic decency of migratory strangers, and I always do what I can to be friendly and entertaining, and to make up for the diminution of creature comforts caused by the addition of another body to an already crowded back seat.

And that pretty much wraps up this inquiry. There are some duodecimo vehicles—motorcycles, with or without sidecars, and bicycles—and their riders can often help to keep your spirits up with a smile and a wave, but only once has one offered me a ride. I took it, of course, even though it was during my first year on the road and I was still carrying a full frame pack and had my guitar in a heavy wooden case. It was a small motorbike, on a lonely stretch of road in Morocco, and only carried me a few miles up the road, but it remains a unique and charming memory, I hope for the cyclist as much as for myself.

A FELLOW MUSICIAN

Meanwhile, we have been off the road too long, and it is time to get moving. After two days in Iowa City, relaxing with my friends, doing some reading, making some music, I was both rested and restless. My host, Dave Moore, was playing at a blues festival in Grinnell on Saturday morning, and I seized the opportunity to get a fifty-mile running start. By eleven o'clock, he had dropped me at the rest area at mile 180, with only another seven hundred miles between me and the Rocky Mountains.

I had a plan, purely provisional but rooted in my fear of getting stuck on the interstate in Nebraska, a fate I have long contemplated with special horror. To other travelers along I-80, Iowa and Nebraska are joined in a single long and flat continuum, but to hitchhikers they are as disparate as heaven and hell. Iowa is the first state you encounter as you head west that allows you to stand on the side of the interstate, cheerfully flashing your thumb at whatever traffic may pass. Nebraska, by contrast, has strict laws against pedestrians on the interstate, and strictly enforces them— and it is an awesomely wide and empty state with entrance ramps that roadside legend decorates with the stripped and desiccated bones of myriad marooned wayfarers.

At least, that is how I have always understood the situation. Prey to the motley superstitions of the road, I absorbed this one from some long-forgotten fellow traveler, and have lived by it ever since. For all I know, Nebraska may in fact be just as friendly and hospitable as any other state. But I took the warning to heart, and have never accepted a ride that would leave me within its far-flung borders. (Such phobias are not uncommon among hitchers. Crossing Canada, I was warned several times not to accept a ride into Wawa, Ontario, famous across the nation as a hitchhikers' graveyard, and I once met a German who traveled regularly to Italy and turned down any ride that would drop him in Switzerland. I never stopped in Wawa, but several times hitched in Switzerland, and while it is true that the Swiss are among the least hospitable people on earth, I always found enough immigrant and tourist traffic to get me through the country.)

The whiff of Iowan freedom was too precious to risk, especially as it provided a first taste of the glories of hitching in the wide-open West. The freedom to walk or stand out on the highway and signal your desires to any passing vehicle is a universal glory of the cowboy states, at least on the northern and central runs. The statute books may say otherwise—on paper, Wyoming has a total ban on hitching—but a loose and situational interpretation of the law is part of the region's treasured pioneer heritage. So once you have passed Illinois or Minnesota, Nebraska is the only place where police will mess with you until you cross the state lines into California or Washington, and if you go by way of Oregon you have free use of the breakdown lane clear through to the Pacific.

My next destination, if the traffic flowed as planned, was Butte, Montana. My projected route would therefore be along I-80 to just outside Omaha, then north on I-29 to Sioux Falls, South Dakota, where I could pick up I-90 and follow it through Spearfish, Sheridan, and Billings into Butte. If it had been full summer, I would have been tempted to follow old Highway 20 as it meanders across northern Nebraska and twists up into Wyoming, passing through Yellowstone and tossing in some moose and geysers for lagniappe. In September, though, I didn't trust the weather on Wyoming's back roads. Down jacket or not, getting stranded at night on top of the Rockies in a rainstorm is no damn joke. Anyway, life is long, and there would be other opportunities. For now, I was counting on the warp and weft of interstates.

The rest area where Dave dropped me was small and nondescript, but what a pleasure to be able to walk undisturbed down its exit ramp, out to whatever spot suited my fancy. I chose a place where the cars coming off the plaza would not yet have picked up speed, but where drivers on the highway would have plenty of time to see me and get over into the breakdown lane. I had been there about five minutes when a pair of state police cars appeared in the distance, drew near, and passed me by without a pause: a minor incident, but such small joys give life its savor— there is nothing like hunger to spice a plain meal, and nothing like a few days of hitchhiking in the East to make one delight in the sight of a passing Iowa patrol car.

Five minutes more and a gray minibus pulled off the interstate, with lettering on its side proclaiming it the property of St. Paul's Lutheran Church. I ran up, opened the front passenger door, and was greeted by a skinny old guy with sky-blue eyes and hair the color of the parched cornfields. "I couldn't leave a fellow musician standing on the side of the road," he said, nodding in agreement with his own comment.

I settled myself in the seat, and took up the conversation: "What do you play?"

"Oh, just about anything I get my hands on. Guitar, mandolin, fiddle, button accordion, concertina . . ."

I told him that I had just left a friend in Iowa City who also played accordion. I had never realized that Iowa was accordion country. "Oh yeah," my driver assured me. "Up where I live, in Walker, they got an accordion repairman up there and he's already got jobs backed up into next year."

His voice was a flat, affectless monotone, and he jumped from thought to thought without any obvious connections. He was on his way to Des Moines, to a bicycle flea market. "They've got every kind of bicycle there, from the 1890s up to the latest models; it's pretty interesting, if you want to come along." He also knew an instrument maker north of town. "You know what a Hardanger fiddle is? They play 'em in Norway. They have extra strings that kind of echo the ones you play. This guy makes 'em, he's one of the only ones in the country that does that. Two thousand five hundred dollars he gets for one instrument." He asked if I'd ever played a concertina. "Easiest instrument in the world. You want to make a chord, you just take a note, then you go two buttons away, and if that doesn't work you go two buttons away from that, and you've got a chord." He was holding up three fingers, to illustrate the method. "Dolly Parton—did you know her assets are worth fifty million dollars?" He paused speculatively, raising his eyebrows: "You know what assets I'm talking about . . ." I could guess. "Your guitar's almost as beat up as Willie Nelson's. His is so beat up it's got a hole in it."

"Still sounds good, though."

"Oh yeah. You ever get a ride from a woman driving alone?"

"Not often, but it happens now and then."

"Any of them ever invite you home with them? I read a story about a young guy out hitchhiking, and a woman picked him up, and then she said she had to stop off at her house for something, and she invited him to come in, sat him in the living room and told him to wait, then she went into her bedroom and came back out without a stitch of clothes on her and said she hadn't had it for a long time and she needed some right that moment. So they did it right there on the couch, and then she took him back out and dropped him off back on the road. Anything like that ever happen to you?"

"Nope."

And thus it went until we reached the last rest area before Des Moines.

A RIDE ACROSS

THE PLAINS

With freedom comes responsibility, which is why it is by no means universally desired. "I can't" is an easier excuse than "I can, but choose not to," and many people are happier feeling constrained than accepting responsibility for their fate. Heavy as the implications of this thought may be, in the present case it is frittered away on a triviality: The freedom to stand out on the highway meant that I had to choose whether to play guitar as I waited or to concentrate all of my energy on hailing a ride. Stuck on rest areas, where I could only hitch the cars that had stopped, I had always had time to play a verse or so between thumbings. Now, there was a constant stream of traffic calling for my attention, but I was also out in the middle of the Great Plains, under a broad blue sky, and how could I not yodel? As so many indecisive characters have done in similar situations, I opted for an uncomfortable compromise: I would strum a couple of chords, then swing out my thumb as I sang, trying to keep my smile intact even on the high notes. I probably presented an absurd and haphazard spectacle, but the only possible observers were passing me at seventy miles an hour and, as long as they didn't choose to stop, their opinions had no relevance. For myself, I was at peace with the universe.

The view stretched uninterrupted to the horizon, fraught with infinite promise, and however compromised, the pioneer myth swirled round me in the dusty breeze. I had escaped the thickly settled, overcivilized East, had acres of clear sky above and of open prairie underfoot, and could stand unmolested on the highway. For the next thousand miles, the mystical alchemy of the road would transform me into a cowboy, surveying an enticing herd of wild mustangs and swinging my thumb like a lariat. And to hell with the perversions of that dream. Don't tell me that the cowboys were all imperialist conquerors, committing genocide as they raped the west. Most of them were poor, adventurous sons-of-bitches trying to get by and get away and, when possible, get a decent drink and enjoy the freedom of the open range. A good many of them spoke Spanish better than English, and plenty of them had roots in Africa or south of the Rio Grande. And some of them were thieves, cheats, and murderers, but there is a big difference between a lone murderer and the U.S. Cavalry. And in those days even generals still led their troops into action, so when an idiot like Custer conducted his campaign of slaughter, he also paid its price—albeit only after extorting a similar price from a lot of better men, not to mention women and children, who had no choice in the matter. Today the cowboy myth has been hijacked by exactly the sort of people who once remained safe in their mansions, buying and selling railroad stock and never setting foot west of the Mississippi. And they still remain safe in their mansions, when not flying around in private jets or demonstrating their pioneer spirit by going on organized hunting trips after stocked-and-released game.

It is long past time to reclaim the American mythology from those who have perverted it to support their lust for a cowed and frightened populace at home and rapacious piracy abroad. Because if you dig through the bullshit, there is a great deal to love and honor about this country. Or maybe I'm the one who's delusional, standing out here in the middle of Iowa, holding onto a dream that's been debased and forgotten, twisted to such a degree that the wild optimism of Crazy Horse and Bob LaFollette has shrunk and walled itself into little bunkers of worried conservatism. I don't believe it, though. Beyond the televised perversions of corporate fearmongers who cannot trust because they are not to be trusted, the plains still welcome me, open-armed as ever, and the roaring iron mustangs leap and gallop west, and no one knows what tomorrow may bring.

I was singing truck driving songs, concocting sympathetic magic to lure a big rig off the road:

The ICC is a-checkin' on down the line,
I'm a little overweight and my log book's way behind,
But nothin' bothers me at night,
    I can dodge all the scales all right,
Six days on the road . . .

And a truck pulled up on my left, coming out of the rest area. The face looking out the window was round, smiling, and unquestionably female. There had to be some mistake. But no, she nodded and tilted her head back, signaling for me to come on. It's an infinitely surprising world.

On Route 80 in the middle of Iowa, you don't need to waste time with a conversation about where the driver is headed. You are both going far enough, and will have plenty of time to sort out the details once you are moving. So I got myself settled in the passenger seat, with my pack on the floor beside me and my guitar nestled safely on the bed in the back, while my host brought us up to cruising speed. Then it was time for the exchange of basic information: I said I was headed to the Pacific Northwest, planning to cut north on 29. She said she was headed to Los Angeles.

So there it was again, the responsibility of freedom. Now I had to decide if I really wanted to take Route 29, or if I wanted to stay with this ride straight across Nebraska. I asked if she was picking up 70 in Denver or sticking with 80 across Wyoming. She said 80 was a better road. I asked if it would be OK for me to ride along into Wyoming. She said, "Sure, no problem."

She had an accent, so I asked where she was from. "The Czech Republic." Her name was Martina, "like the tennis player." She was in her early thirties, and she looked more like a European college student than like an American truck driver. She was sturdily built, wearing round-rimmed glasses, a pastel pink T-shirt, and a loose, wraparound summer skirt that fell slightly open when she moved her leg forward to hit the brake. Not seductive, just relaxed and unconscious about it. I said I had been in Prague once, back in the early 1980s. "Oh, during the communists." She had been a kid at that time, and it was only a rather vague memory, displaced by successive shifts of politics and geography. She had been in the United States for eight years already. She came over with her husband, an American she met while he was in the army, stationed in Germany. She was working there as a waitress. Before that, she had traveled a lot, hitchhiking all over Europe, even down to Spain and Italy. She had gotten divorced a few years ago, but they were still good friends. She had been driving trucks for two and a half years. She had a fiancé who was also a truck driver, and also Czech. He drove for the same company, out of Chicago, and they sometimes made runs together, but it was much better money if they drove separately. You only got an extra $150 for a second driver. So they usually drove one week together, then one apart. She did the run out to L.A. pretty often. This time she was hauling a load for IBM; she thought it was computer bodies, but was not sure.

Apparently, there are quite a few Czechs driving out of Chicago, part of the recent Eastern European migration. We were barely past Des Moines when Martina suddenly reached for the mike on her CB, flicked it on, and began firing off questions in what I assumed was Czech. As it happened, I was slightly off. "He's a Polish truck," she explained, after signing off. "I see him coming the other way; I know the company from Chicago."

"So you speak Polish?"

"It is not so different, and there are many Polish truck drivers, so we all learn enough to ask about the weather and if the scales are open or where the police are." Channel twenty-five on the CB is now the Slavic band, she tells me, with all the conversation in Polish and Russian.

That is quite a change from the trucking culture of the "Convoy" days, but even with this new blood the CB seems to be going the way of the eight-track, another victim of evolving technology. For much of the long ride across Nebraska, Martina chatted on her cell phone. She explained that she would have no signal once she got up in the mountains, so she had to talk with her fiancé and also with another Czech driver who was on his way back from L.A. on the same route. I had not considered what a difference cell phones would make in the trucking world. It must drive some of the older guys crazy, that their boss or their wife can now reach them out on the highway. The old way was often lonely, but like the sea, it attracted men who liked that sensation. There is an odd security that comes with being in the wilderness or out in open water, where no one can touch or hold you. Irresistible as cell phones and e-mail may be, they bring with them the irritating knowledge that every lifeline is also a bond, tying you to home, to work, to your loved ones—not a bad thing, maybe, overall, but nonetheless another string attached.

Martina gave no sign of sharing such misgivings. She probably had a cell phone before she ever thought of driving a truck. And she is a new kind of driver, unlike any I had ridden with before. Crossing into Nebraska, she had to pull into a weigh station, and since her paperwork did not mention a passenger I had to hide in the back of the cab. I have hidden this way so many times that I start toward the back automatically as a driver turns off, pulling the curtain shut behind me. But this was the first time I found the driver's bed covered with stuffed animals: they were lined up neatly by the pillow, starting with a huge blue dog and descending by size to an eight-inch-tall Smoky the Bear, and they kept me company till the officials waved us through and we were back on the highway.

Martina enjoyed her job, but she was not caught up in it as a way of life, or even as a long-term career. For now, it was fine. She liked the travel, and told me that in nice weather she often leaves the highway and explores back roads, seeing as much of the country as possible. No American-born trucker has ever suggested to me that he might leave the interstate for a touristic detour. She was also proud to be one of the few women making runs on their own. Plenty of women drive semis these days, but almost all of them took up the trade to partner with their husbands. The trucking companies began encouraging this back in the 1980s, because they found it made for safer driving and fewer complaints. A long-haul trucker is sometimes out for weeks, and can get to feeling like the Flying Dutchman, sailing under a curse that keeps home always tantalizingly out of reach. The boss will send him to Oregon, say, promising to find a return load that will take him home to Oklahoma, but unfortunately the only loads available will be destined for the East Coast. So off he goes to New York, only to find that the only southbound loads are going to Florida, and then all the Florida loads are earmarked for Chicago, which has a load for New York again, and there a load for Houston almost takes him home, except that the only load out of there is a rush job that has to get to Washington, D.C. This kind of thing is getting rarer, but over the years I've heard drivers bitching in truck stops across the country, cursing the dispatcher and drunkenly wondering if their wives would still be there when they finally made it home. So now the wives often come along, and not only are there fewer complaints but there is less drinking and fooling around. There are some young couples, marrying and starting a life together on the road, but most of the women you see are older, grandmotherly figures who joined their husbands after twenty years at home raising the kids and grumbling their own complaints about the vagaries of the trucking routes. I see them only at a distance, up behind the wheel or walking across parking lots. They will never pick up a hitchhiker, first because they already have a companion in the cab, and secondly because they have no interest in inviting an unknown tramp into what has become a neat, respectable home that only incidentally is hauling several tons of freight across the continent.

Martina had drifted into trucking by chance, meeting other Czech drivers in Chicago who were willing to take her along and teach her the trade, then to partner with her once she had a license. The company hired her strictly as a relief driver, and it was more than a year before her boss would let her take a load out on her own. "He asked me what was I going to do if I broke down on the road, a woman by myself. I said, 'I'd do just the same as the men do: call a repair service.'" By now, she had done enough runs that he had stopped worrying, but she was very conscious of being a rarity. In all her time on the road, she had met only one other woman driving single, at a truck stop near Barstow.

She was headed for Barstow now, pushing hard because she wanted to sleep there Sunday night and get into L.A. early Monday morning before the traffic got bad. Tonight, she planned to sleep in a lot outside Rawlins, halfway across Wyoming. That would be almost two thousand miles in two days, some eighteen hours straight driving from Chicago to Rawlins, then another twelve or thirteen from Rawlins to Barstow. Regulations allow no more than twelve hours driving on each shift, then mandate an eight-hour rest, but she thought that was stupid. As she explained, it forced people out of their natural biorhythms and made them cycle around the clock, sleeping at different hours each day. She had found that she got more tired if she tried to keep to that schedule than if she drove all day and slept at night—and what's more, she thought most drivers had the same problem and that was one of the reasons they fell asleep and had wrecks. So her solution was to push on through, pausing only for gas and occasional bathroom breaks, and to sleep her regular night-time hours. Food she barely worried about. When we stopped for ten minutes at a highway rest stop, I came back from the toilets to find her microwaving a couple of plastic containers of homemade chicken noodle soup— one for each of us—and that was all she ate that day. "My boss told me that when you're driving you have to sleep regularly and eat regularly, and if you can't do both you should at least do one or the other." She had picked sleeping, or at least that was her official choice. As far as I could tell, she was not overdoing either.

So we rolled on, across the meditative plains of Nebraska. What better place to contemplate the vastness of the country, of travel, of life, than this placid infinity of farmland. What better study of the subtle variations that hold the world together: no two barns quite alike, each clump of trees a unique island, yet all of it repeating, cornfield after cornfield, to the perfectly straight line where gold and blue meet at the horizon. There is no way to travel quickly across the great open spaces between the Mississippi and the Rockies: a mile a minute of this steadily unfurling, uniformly patterned fabric is a journey back to drifting herds and ox-drawn wagons traversing it by months and years. It is a becalmed ocean, over which a drowsy sleeper drifts timelessly, then, yawning and stretching, finds that he has somehow risen five thousand feet above its eastern bed, and is surrounded by the chill air and naked hillsides of the high plains.

A racing banjo, a lightly leaping mandolin, and a raw mountain tenor provided the perfect soundtrack for the journey. Martina's family had all played bluegrass, back in Czechoslovakia, and now she flipped cassette after cassette into the player, treating me to the complete history of the Fragment Band, her favorite group from home. One tape in English, one in Czech, alternating hour by hour, all with the same highballing rhythms and tight, Kentucky harmonies. She plays mandolin herself, and also bass guitar, and is taking a week's vacation in October to go to the International Bluegrass Music Association convention in Louisville, Kentucky. The Fragment Band will be there, a highlight of their current American tour, and she is making sure that she will not miss them. "My boss is angry. He says, 'Why do you have to take a whole week, why can't you just go for the weekend of the convention?' But I know that if I don't take the whole week I will end up stuck in L.A. waiting for a return load, and I will miss it all. It happens so often, I buy tickets for a concert and then I can't go because I am somewhere else. So this time I make sure."

The sky ahead of us turned bright orange, then dimmed to pink, then gray, outlining our first view of the Rockies. Another two hours and we would reach Cheyenne. I still had no fixed plan. If I cut north on I-25, then I could turn off on state highway 20 or 14 toward Yellowstone or catch I-90 past the Little Bighorn into Billings and on to Butte. That would mean spending the night either in Cheyenne or somewhere outside of town, near the highway intersection. Cheyenne itself did not attract me much, but a night on the high plains, watching the stars and listening to coyotes blending their howls with the rumble of the highway was a romantic image, and would give me an early start. Only it might get too cold, this high up. And I had the option of riding along with Martina into Rawlins and catching 287 north from there, or even spending the night in a truck stop motel and then going on with her to Utah. None of the choices was bad, and none had to be made before Cheyenne. So I listened to Czech bluegrass and watched the shadows of the mountains, and waited for the highway gods to send a sign.

ANOTHER NIGHT

ON THE ROAD

As we came up on Cheyenne, a light drizzle of rain speckled the windshield. Not a good omen for sleeping out, and when we pulled into a truck stop, the woman at the register said there was heavier rain expected by midnight. So I'd get a motel in Rawlins.

While the tank filled, Martina put on a pair of canvas gloves the size of fielder's mitts and gave the truck a basic checkup. Stretching my legs alongside, I was struck by the contrast in scale between truck and trucker: it was like watching someone groom a dinosaur. The hood on a semi opens forward, tilting grill and all away from the cab, a ponderous hunk of metal that must weigh many hundreds of pounds, and yet is so nicely balanced that it can be raised with one hand. Martina opened it, then climbed up and leaned over until she was almost inside the engine and pulled out the dipstick. It was a little low, so she opened a compartment on the side of the cab, behind the driver's door, and got out a big plastic jug of oil, climbed back up and topped it off. Then, from the same compartment, she got out a heavy wooden baton and circled the trailer, thumping all the tires. I have watched this mysterious ritual many times over the years, and always wondered what exactly the drivers were thumping for. This time I got my answer. One of the inside rear tires had sprung a leak, but since the wheels on a semi are grouped in pairs, a soft tire is held off the ground and does not look any different from a full one. Hence the thumping.

Now Martina had to walk over to the garage and find a repairman. We were lucky: It was a slow night and they could take us immediately. We climbed back in the cab, and she drove around to the garage's main entrance and eased the truck into the slip. After poking around, the mechanic announced that the job would take him about twenty minutes. Forced to pause, Martina decided to fill the time with a shower. She offered to treat me to one as well, but I figured I would wait until I reached the motel, where I could relax and luxuriate in the hot water, rather than hurrying to meet her schedule. Instead I used the telephone, trying unsuccessfully to reach various friends in the Northwest. I was pretty hungry, but didn't want to take a chance on ordering any food, in case Martina was ready to leave before it arrived. Sure enough, she was out before I got off the phone, and by the time we had walked back across the lot the truck was ready.

Two more hours and we were passing Rawlins. Martina knew a truck stop that had a hotel, so we turned off at that exit, but by then it was midnight and the lot was completely full, besides which the desk clerk said a single room would cost me sixty dollars, which was twice what Martina had guessed. Martina said she was sorry, that I would be welcome to sleep in the cab if it had two beds, but unfortunately it didn't. I was surprised that she would even consider letting me stay in the cab, and instantly seized the opening, saying that if it was really all right with her, I could sleep in my seat. She said it was no problem for her, but I wouldn't be able to get any sleep there; her partner had tried it once, and it was too uncomfortable. I said that, tired as I was, it would be comfortable enough. So that was that. We headed west another few miles, found a lot that had some free spaces, and parked for the night.

Of the sleeping conditions, there is little to add. Martina provided me with a couple of pillows and a blanket, and I propped myself up as best I could. It was not ideal, but I managed well enough, shifting between two basic positions: sometimes I leaned against the door with my legs stretched toward the floor in the middle of the cab, and sometimes scrunched on my side with my feet up on the dashboard. The heater was on, which combined with the long day's travel to make me drowsy, and I had the satisfying reassurance of many hundreds of miles behind me. I was aware that it would make a racier story if I were back in the bed with Martina, but literary fillips aren't everything. The romance of this trip was truck cabs and the gentle hum of diesel engines in the Wyoming darkness, with a third of the continent still ahead. So I slipped in and out of sleep, cozy and tranquil, till the gray predawn light poked my eyes open. Then I quietly opened the door and hurried over to the truck stop to get some food.

It was six thirty and Martina had said she wanted to get on the road by seven o'clock—though, keeping to Chicago time, she called it eight —which left just enough time for a proper truck stop breakfast. I sat at the counter for faster service, and ordered the "Big Three Special," three eggs over medium with three slices of bacon, three sausage links, three pancakes, wheat toast, and hash browns. There were two waitresses behind the counter, one about forty with black hair teased up in a sort of semi-bouffant, the other maybe twenty-five, with a sand-colored ponytail, slim and pretty in a bored, small-town way. They were talking about black widow spiders. "I don't even like to think about them," the younger one was saying. "If I thought there was any in my house, I'd fumigate."

"Then you better just stay out of your attic," the older one advised, with a thin smile. "They're in every house in Rawlins. If you've got anything stored and don't move it around every few weeks you get them in there. There's no point fumigating, 'cause they just come right back. Anyway, they're good; they keep the mosquitoes down."

The young waitress shuddered, exaggerating to make sure no one missed it. "I'd rather have a few mosquito bites."

There were a dozen or so truckers at the tables, smoking cigarettes with their coffee. The guy sitting next to me told the older waitress that he was headed for Seattle. I considered asking if he'd carry me, but kept quiet. He was already paying his bill, and I had only eaten half my breakfast. Besides, I didn't know if Martina was awake yet, or if I would be able to get into the cab and get my stuff. And the sky was clear, I was on top of the Rockies, and after a whole day spent in a truck cab I was looking forward to standing out on the highway for a while, breathing mountain air and taking my chances.

RED DESERT AND
LITTLE AMERICA

The cab was locked when I got back, so I stretched and slouched around until Martina turned up, freshly showered and ready for another day's driving. It was a perfect morning, warm and clear, and the country seemed bigger than ever from the height of a semi cab. Soon we would pass Red Desert, where I once spent five days marooned with a Renault drive-away, waiting for a new axle from Salt Lake City. It was a true-life excerpt from a bad pulp novel, featuring Joe, the mechanic; his wife Ronette, the waitress; Joe's mother, who did the cooking and got on Ronette's nerves; and a heavy-equipment operator named Tex, whose wife had left him, as a result of which he was drinking himself to death in the otherwise empty motel. There was also a guy living alone by the other gas station across the highway, but I never saw him. When I broke down, I increased Red Desert's population by twenty percent. I had pulled off to get some coffee and a moment's rest in the middle of the worst blizzard I have ever driven through, and it was pure luck that the axle finally ceased functioning in the parking lot rather than out on the highway where I would have promptly been hit by a semi, or left the car and frozen to death. Instead, Ronette closed down the restaurant and we all drove into Rawlins to celebrate St. Patrick's Day. I brought my guitar and played Hank Williams songs at the bar in exchange for shots of Jameson's Irish whiskey, and woke up the next morning fully dressed on one of the motel beds, then spent the next five days walking around the desert looking for arrowheads, wishing I could just leave the damn car and hitchhike east. It is always a pleasure to roll past Red Desert.

On up the road, we passed the aftermath of a nasty accident: a semi was pulled over in the breakdown lane and a car lay at a weird angle on the grass of the median strip, its right side crushed, with an ambulance and two police cars behind it. It's always safer to be in the truck. Though in Nebraska we'd passed a place where a semi had taken out a bridge support on the eastbound side, shutting down the whole highway. Intimations of mortality; the stove boats and shipwrecks of the plains. You wince and drive on.

My plans had changed again. The lot where we had slept was ten miles west of Rawlins, and to cut north from there I would have had to backtrack, hoping to get a ride to the middle of town, then walk out and pick up state highway 287. Martina had made the unprecedented offer to add twenty-five miles to her route by turning off 80 before Salt Lake City and taking me up to Ogden, which would give me a clear shot into Idaho, but there was a smaller, prettier-looking route, state highway 30 up to Pocatello, which she said a lot of truckers used as a shortcut, and it seemed like the perfect diversion for a day of fair-weather hitching.

We stopped for a bathroom break at Little America, a service plaza so big that it is on the maps as a town. Hundreds of trucks idled in the lot, and just for the fun of it I asked Martina if I could get on her CB and try to scare up a ride. I have heard dozens of stories of truck drivers passing hitchhikers along from one to the next by way of the CB, but it had happened to me only once, and that was back in the 1970s. Martina wanted to go into the restaurant and make a phone call, and she said I was welcome to use the radio as much as I wanted. Just push the sliding switch on the side of the mouthpiece to talk, then release it to listen: "Hi there, I'm a guitar player, just pulled into Little America with a semi headed towards L.A., and I'm looking for a driver who would be willing to take me up into Idaho."

The first try got no response, so I waited five minutes and gave it another shot. This time someone asked, "What part of Idaho?"

"It doesn't really matter; I'm headed toward Vancouver, so I can either go up 15 to Butte and pick up 90 or go over on 84."

Dead silence. I should have been specific. Then, if he happened to be going where I said, he might have carried me. I probably sounded like I just wanted to get into someone's cab. But I really didn't care which route I took, and since I was just as happy taking my chances on the road, it felt wrong to over-strategize my CB approach.

Martina got back and took me three more miles, to where Route 30 went off on the right. I used the time to give the CB one more try: "I'm a guitar player, headed towards Idaho. I'll be standing at the turnoff for Route 30. If anyone's headed that way, look me over, and if I look OK I'd appreciate it if you'd give me a lift."

Then Martina dropped me at the exit, and I started walking down the ramp toward 30. I hadn't made it fifty yards before another semi pulled over in front of me.

RUSSIAN

I didn't bother to ask where the truck was going—any ride up 30 was fine with me. Except that, as it turned out, this truck wasn't going up 30 at all; instead of picking me up as he slowed for the exit, as I had assumed, he had pulled off 80 just for me, and now pulled on again. "Where are you going?" he asked, and when I told him I was headed for the Northwest he said, "I am going to Seattle." He had a thick accent, so I asked where he was from. "Russian. No American truck driver stopping for you here." True enough; trucks almost never pull over when they are going full-tilt down the interstate.

His name was Sergei, and he was from the Ural Mountains, "Very beautiful country." He had been in America only two years, and driving a truck for a year and a half. It was a new experience for him. In Russia, he had been a radio engineer, but he did not speak enough English to look for a radio job here. So for the moment he was driving, and enjoying the chance to get familiar with the landscape. He mimed sightseeing, putting his hand up to shield his eyes and gazing out toward the snow-capped peaks in the distance. "I go everywhere. I know more U.S.A. than Russia."

He did a lot of miming, making up for words he couldn't find. He was obviously a talkative, entertaining fellow in his own language, and while his English was serviceable, it was insufficiently colorful to suit his taste. He had tried taking classes to make it better, but he was on the road too much. His kids all spoke good English, though. He had three, aged fourteen, seventeen, and eighteen, two boys and the middle one was a girl. They had all come over together, after his wife died. "Her stomach," he said, rubbing his own and grimacing. "Cancer. It was very bad."

I mentioned that my girlfriend had lived for a while in St. Petersburg. "Ah!" He beamed. "Very beautiful. No city like this in U.S.A." I nodded, and said something about it being very historic. "Yes! History. Here, no history. In America, all building wood, wood, wood. In Russia—stone!" He held up a clenched fist, symbolizing the majestic power of Russian architecture.

It was a thoroughly enjoyable ride. Sergei was a charming character, a solid father taking care of his kids, but proud to still be a rebel. The pioneer spirit, yet again. He had a pair of black, wraparound sunglasses that he kept taking off and putting on without any apparent relationship to the brightness of the light, and a green sleeveless T-shirt with what looked like some kind of heavy metal logo on it. He kept the tape player turned up high when he wasn't talking, blaring Russian hard rock. He would sing along with the songs, tapping on the steering wheel and looking cool in his shades, then a question would occur to him and he would reach for the volume dial and resume the conversation.

"What are you doing for work?"

"I play some guitar, and also I am a writer."

"A writer?" He grinned. "In back I have forty thousand books." He gestured toward the trailer. "Very, very heavy."

We crossed into Utah, and picked up 84 toward Ogden. A few miles past the junction, Sergei began rummaging through a box on the floor beside him, then pulled out a camera and handed it to me. "Now, you work," he said. There was a small widening in the road on the right, marked Scenic Bypass, and he pulled over, filling it completely. We got out, and he pointed at a curious rock formation across the road: a smooth, white groove between rounded lips, running down the length of the hillside. A sign proclaimed it The Devil's Slide, though I could imagine it had been given other names over the years. "Nothing like this in Russia," Sergei said. He walked back with the camera and composed a picture, then waved me over to act as photographer and went to pose with his elbow on the front of the cab: "Take me, the truck, the rock." I took two shots, just in case. Then he said, "OK. Work over." And on we rolled toward Idaho.

We passed a truck coming the other way, with a woman at the wheel and a man in the passenger seat. "In Russia you don't see this," Sergei said. "Russian woman is not driving trucks. American woman . . ." he shook his head, looking mystified.

"Not just American women." I felt honor-bound to stand up for Martina. "My last ride, the driver was from the Czech Republic, and she was a woman. Driving alone. She has been driving for more than two years."

Sergei made a face. "This is not right, I don't like. Woman should be woman, and man should be man."

Sergei was making the best of his situation, but there was a lot about America that troubled or puzzled him. Some things were just the way he had expected them to be, but others were surprising and inexplicable. For example, he had always heard that America was the most modern, efficient country in the world, and he didn't understand why in some ways it seemed so backward. He was especially disappointed in the schools: "My daughter, she learns mathematics. In Russia, her marks are all four, four, four. Here, right away, five, five, five! I am shocked. This year, I send the two young children to Russia for school. I tell them they can come back to America when they have college. College is good here. But how can this be? Russia schools very good; here very bad. So why do people live better here? I don't understand."

The hard rock tape was finished, and he replaced it with a tape by a generic-sounding Russian pop singer named Linda, then with Pink Floyd's *Dark Side of the Moon*. That brought back memories for both of us: for me, of dozens of European hitchhiking rides in the 1970s; for him, of his college years. "1980. This was new. We all listened." Apparently it had taken the record a few extra years to breach the Iron Curtain. Then came a tape of hip-hop, first in English, then in French, though the French had so much slang in it that at first I thought it must be Russian. Sergei was equally unsure for a moment: "I think Russian . . . No, no, yes, it's French. I don't know this. I play this to connect with my children."

The oldest son was in college in Seattle, and Sergei saw him often, but the younger kids had flown to Russia three weeks ago, at the start of the new school year, and he missed them. "My young boy, he call me this week. I tell him he can come back in the summer." They were living with his wife's brother, in his old home town. He told me the name of the town, but I didn't get it, though he repeated it twice. "It is very old town, very beautiful." He thought for a moment, then it came to him: "Oh yes! Maybe you know: 1960, American spy plane. We shoot down." He mimed a man holding the straps of a parachute, then fluttered his right hand slowly toward his lap, like a pilot drifting to earth. "Come down in field. Farmer arrest him." He mimed marching, and flashed me a wide smile: "Big celebration!" (My memories of the Gary Powers affair were pretty vague, but I later worked out that Sergei's town was Ekaterinburg.)

Crossing into Idaho, I had to hide in the back while we went through the weigh station. Sergei shook his head. "In Russia, no scales." He waggled the wheel happily: "Just drive!" Wherever truckers come from, regulations are a pet complaint. And frankly, hitchhikers share this view. As we emerged from the weigh station, Sergei explained that he was sorry, but he would have to stop and sleep in another two hours, at mile ninety-five. He would have driven twelve hours by then, and his company was very strict. Meanwhile, we made a brief stop in a rest area and had some lunch, big slabs of ham and cheese on bread that Sergei cut from a loaf he kept in one of the back cabinets. This seems to be one thing all the immigrant truckers have in common: Mexican or Slavic, they prefer to bring their own food and eat sandwiches rather than spending money on truck stop fare. It's cheaper, faster, and probably a good deal healthier.

We were still pretty high up, but the terrain had flattened out. Sergei had the hard rock playing again, and what with the lunch and the warmth of the heater I began to drowse. At first, I fought it, but after I nodded off for the third or fourth time, Sergei shook my arm and gestured toward the bed: "Go sleep. No problem." It would be another hour and a half, and I had no idea where I would end up that night, so I thanked him and stretched out on top of his blanket. He offered to turn off the music, but I said it was fine. And it was. I didn't sleep much, but it felt good to be horizontal for a change, and by the time Sergei pulled off at a truck stop southeast of Boise, I was ready for whatever came next.

THE MELTING POT

As I walked the block or so from the truck stop to the highway entrance, I counted how many immigrant drivers had picked me up in the past few days. It was a striking change from previous trips across the country: My first day had included the Pole, the Chinese couple, and Arturo—though strictly speaking he was not an immigrant, since he still lived in Mexico. The evangelist had been my only native English-speaker on that run. The next two days, all my drivers had been native-born, but I was off the interstate, riding through Midwestern farm country. Once I was back on 80, I'd had two immigrants to one born American. It sure didn't use to be that way. In fact, in all my previous trips around the United States, I can't remember getting one ride from a foreigner. And it had to be more than pure coincidence.

Once again, hitchhiking was putting a finger on the pulse of the country. The last few years have seen an incredible influx of new blood to the United States. According to census figures, twice as many people arrived between 1990 and 2002 as in the 1980s, and the eighties already had double the numbers of the sixties or seventies. By now, about twelve percent of the country's inhabitants come from someplace else—and those are just the official figures, which probably run significantly below the real numbers, since so many are living here illegally and prefer not to answer the door when anyone official-looking comes around. You have to go back to 1931 to find that many foreign-born residents, and the last comparable influx came before World War I.

I remember the first time I heard somebody speaking a foreign language on the street in my home town, and I was probably ten years old. These days, my old high school has native speakers of over fifty different languages. That's around Boston, a port city that has always been more cosmopolitan than most places in the middle of the country, but if there are any corners of the United States that don't number some recent arrivals among their residents, they would have to be pretty remote. Even in the 1980s, I heard a Hmong Laotian radio program broadcasting out of Missoula, Montana. Mexicans are all over the West, Midwest, and South, working factory and farm jobs. Eastern Europeans have headed for the cities where their compatriots settled a hundred years ago, flowing into Pittsburgh and Chicago, Cleveland, New York, and Los Angeles. The West Coast remains the proverbial land of opportunity, with Asians, Latinos, Persians, Africans, and all sorts of other folks who have heard of California even if they know nothing else about America. Disneyland! I once spent a few days in Mexico with a guy who thought Disneyland was a separate country, in the ocean off the California coast. But the West's lure reaches back at least to the 1800s: the gold rush, the land rush, the mythology so potent that Robert Johnson, down in the Mississippi Delta, would sing of going out "to the land of California, to my sweet home Chicago."

Most of the immigrants arrive in cities, and any American city dweller has long since gotten used to their company, but by now they have spread out through the capillaries of the body politic. Sociologists can debate the meaning of this transfusion, theorizing about whether it will be good or bad for our jobs, our democracy, our culture—as if our culture has ever been anything but a culture of immigrants since the first colonists took over the joint—but for hitchhikers, the newly multicultural highways are the most promising development of my lifetime. I don't know why the immigrants stop so readily: maybe they are less caught up in the paranoid wagon-circling that has a lot of native-born Americans sealing themselves off in gated communities and big, empty SUVs. Immigration is fired by optimism: you go somewhere in the expectation that it will be better than the place you are leaving. Maybe that same optimism carries over when it comes to encountering strangers by the side of the road. Or maybe picking up roadside Americans is just part of the natural urge to meet new people and make new friends as part of your life in a new country. Or it may be that on the all-but-abandoned roadsides of twenty-first century America, I look like the last vestige of a romantic dream that people carry with them from back home, the lone rambler with his guitar, living out his fabled freedom in the vast open spaces seen in so many American movies. I'm on the road because I am still a romantic, a dreamer, and a believer in the common decency of the average human being—so in my way I suppose I too am a kind of migrant. Maybe these drivers sense that we are all in the same boat. Or maybe they come from countries where hitchhiking is still common, and I am just triggering a dormant reflex.

Or maybe this is all pure happenstance, and my next trip will not include a single ride from anyone born outside the United States. Anything is possible, and it wouldn't be the first time I built an elaborate theory on air. In any case, as immigrant follows immigrant, I can't help feeling like I'm getting a taste of a new America, and from what I can see, the change is all for the good.

THE WHITENESS
OF THE DRIVERS

While musing on the varied nationalities of the drivers, it is hard not to remark one glaring absence: I'd had rides this trip from WASPs, Eastern Europeans, Asians, and a Latino, but so far none from African-Americans, Africans, Haitians . . . And it isn't just this trip. In my first few years of hitching back and forth between the coasts, I never once got a ride from a black driver. I ascribed this to the racism that pervades American culture, and often wondered how different the experience of a black hitchhiker would be. I picked up a couple of black hitchhikers in my touring days, one in Iowa headed for Lincoln, Nebraska, and one in Albuquerque who rode with me all the way to Los Angeles, but the first guy didn't do much talking and the second said he had never hitchhiked before, so they couldn't solve that mystery. Then I went down South for a change, and the mystery disappeared—or maybe it just got more complicated. In any case, once I hit Georgia I got as many rides from black drivers as from white.

Of course, there is a huge difference between race relations in the North and in the South, neatly summed up in Dick Gregory's dichotomy: "In the South they [white people] don't care how close you get as long as you don't get too big, and in the North they don't care how big you get as long as you don't get too close." Racist or not, southerners do not tend to avoid people of what in American terms are considered the "opposite" race, while northerners often do. So that may account for some of the difference in who picks up hitchhikers. But there was another thing that I had never thought about until that first run below the Mason-Dixon Line: up north, black people live in cities. Chicago, New York, and Boston have big, longstanding African-American neighborhoods, but in the outlying rural areas you will not see a black face. In the South, it's the rural areas that often have the thickest black population. Mississippi, goddamn—some of the Delta counties are still more than seventy percent black, even after decades of emigration to St. Louis and Chicago. Since on that trip through the South I was keeping off the interstates and sticking to local roads, and since country folk are on the road every day just to do their shopping or get to their jobs, and rural life encourages you to help out your neighbors in a way that city life does not, it was hardly surprising that I saw a lot more black drivers, or that some of them stopped for me.

In the rest of the country, where "urban" has become a racial euphemism, you see few black drivers on the highway, and especially not steering their own cars along the interstate across Wyoming or Idaho. Out here, most of the black drivers are in trucks. Not all, but the trucking population has a much higher proportion of African-Americans than the tourist or business traffic have. Which is not to say that the trucking world is a paradise of interracial harmony. Like the northern cities, the world of the trucks remains quite thoroughly segregated. If you see a black truck driver, you can generally assume that his partner is black too, and if he is sitting at a table with a couple of other drivers, so are they. White drivers likewise, and Mexican drivers, who are getting to be more common—though there's a linguistic issue there as well, as with the Russians and the Poles—also gather in their own groups. I have sometimes asked black truckers for lifts, without any success so far, but if a black friend wanted hitchhiking advice, I would point them out as a good bet. Frankly, though, no black friend has ever shown the slightest interest in hitchhiking. It's hard enough for a black man just to flag down a taxi in his home town.

We're living in a weird country, no doubt about it. My mother was driving from Boston to Cape Cod one evening about ten years ago, and passed two black men standing beside a car that had broken down, waving their thumbs. She stopped, of course, She was seventy years old and grew up at a time when you pulled over for stranded motorists. So they got into the car and she took them to the next exit and found an open gas station. And, as they were leaving, one of the men came over to her window, and said, "Thank you very much for helping us out—but don't you ever, ever do that again." And what's the moral of that story?

America's race issues just keep on keeping on, despite all the demographic shifts of the last few decades. The children of those

Russians and Poles will be white, native-born Americans. The Asians are almost white in most cities, just as we Jews have been for a long time now—not white enough to be elected president, but white enough that no one much notices which neighborhoods we move into or gets nervous if we are walking behind them on a dark night. As for the Mexicans, they are going to completely change the United States—a tanned, Spanish-speaking people on their way to being a majority in a lot of areas and with their own country right next door to keep old ties strong. Once again, hitchhiking takes us to the heart of the matter: America is changing at a great pace for everyone else, but rides from black drivers are no more common than they were thirty years ago. Extrapolate from there, and you'll find that for a lot of people the world isn't changing much at all.

The wandering thoughts of a drowsy wanderer, walking back out to the interstate. Now I've reached the entrance ramp and had best focus on the business at hand, which is getting through Boise and into Oregon before dark.

CORVETTE

It was six years since I'd hitched in Idaho, but my memory was that it was as permissive as the rest of the west. A lot of easterners have gotten a weird idea about the state, reading about the neo-Nazi enclaves and survivalist compounds in Idaho and Montana and concluding that the region is ferociously right wing and conservative. In fact, it is ferociously maverick. There are plenty of conservatives and racists, but the dominant political impulse still seems to be, "Don't fuck with me and I won't fuck with you." That pioneer spirit, again. It can get ugly as hell, but it is quite unlike the racism and conservatism of the Old South, East, or Midwest, which is rooted in a troglodyte distrust of all outsiders. The mountain states are hard to figure out, because a lot of people here are dead set against being figured out, or typed, or grouped with anyone but the folks they want to be grouped with. So they aren't big on laws that limit freedoms of expression, like for example signaling with your thumb that you'd like them to stop and give you a lift—though they're liable to exercise their own freedom to drive on past. Eternal vigilance, bucko. I'll watch out for myself, you watch out for yourself, and everything will be just fine.

The sign at the foot of the highway entrance ramp just pointed west, and didn't bother to include any No Hitchhiking notices or pictures of pedestrians in red circles with a line through them. So up I went, and was walking toward what looked like the perfect spot when a red Corvette convertible whipped past, squealed to a stop just up the road, then reversed toward me at frightening speed. This was getting to be too damn easy.

The driver jumped out and began shifting luggage around. "It's gonna be tight, but I think we can work this out." He opened the trunk and stowed away a bag that had been sitting on the passenger seat, then wedged my pack in beside it. There was still a cooler on the floor, but I managed to squeeze in with my feet on top of it and my guitar between my knees, and we squealed back onto the highway. It wasn't very comfortable, and I didn't know where he was going, but I wasn't about to turn down a ride in a convertible sports car because of incidental details.

The driver was wearing a powder blue sweater and a jaunty yachting cap. He was coming from Sun Valley, where he had spent the weekend with a group of friends, "just hangin' out, playin' some tunes." As a guitar-totin' hitchhiker, I was part of his weekend vibe. "I used to be a real hippie, back in the sixties. Man, I used to hitchhike all over the place. Now I'm president of the second-largest corporation in Boise—but I still play Dylan songs and smoke dope. Life is good."

The stereo system was playing a Dylan tribute album. The Bose stereo system, as he hastened to point out. With twelve CDs stacked in it, fully programmable from the dashboard. "You never heard sound like that before from a car stereo, did you?"

No indeed.

"The good life, man. But you know, I don't need all of this. I have a daughter that's eighteen, and when she graduates college I'm gonna drop out again."

I imagined him dropping out, maybe to a yacht in the Caribbean. The Jimmy Buffett lifestyle, complete with bales of Jamaican ganja and blondes in bikinis who looked like his daughter's college pals. The good life.

He held to a steady eighty-five miles per hour, except when the radar detector on the dashboard signaled impending speed traps, and we barely had time to hear a half-dozen tunes before we were on the outskirts of Boise. He offered to take me into town, but rush hour was starting and he didn't offer to take me out to the other side—I hinted, but he wasn't picking up on it—and I had no interest in standing in the middle of a traffic jam, even if the cops would let me. So I got out at the last rest stop before the city limits and he roared off on his merry way.

RUSSIAN REDUX

I was looking for a truck this time. Not that I would turn down
a nice, fast car, but I wanted someone who would get me
through to Oregon. It was already four thirty, and the Corvette
owner had warned me that a cold front was coming in and the
temperature was expected to drop below freezing tonight. That
meant I needed to sleep indoors. In some countries, I might have
looked for a ride with a local who would invite me home for the
night—France and Italy are both good for that—but you can't
expect tourist hospitality in your homeland. (Foreigners who have
hitched in the United States often tell me about all the people who
took them home for meals, or to spend the night, or insisted on
making long detours to show them local sights, but I have found
such experiences vanishingly rare.) I was probably going to end

up in a motel. One night's paid sleep in the whole cross-country journey averaged out to a pretty cheap trip. In a perfect world, the motel would be another 250 miles down the road, in Hermiston, Oregon, where 82 branched off toward Seattle. That way, I could get up in the morning and catch a through ride across the state line and on to the coast. Washington is not much fun for hitching, or at least it wasn't the last time I came through, which come to think of it was twenty years ago. Back then, the cops had zero tolerance for people standing out on the highway, and I had no reason to think they had mellowed in the intervening decades.

Meanwhile, most of the passing traffic was just going into Boise, at least if I could judge by the Idaho plates. I decided I would stand on the highway for half an hour and see what came, and if I didn't catch anything decent I would work the rest area cab by cab until I found a truck headed my way.

As usual, I positioned myself where I could get traffic off either the rest area or the highway, and resumed my half-assed musical essays between thumbings. I managed one song, then glanced over my shoulder and saw a truck stopped a couple of hundred yards past me. I hadn't seen him pull over, but he hadn't been there two minutes earlier, and it might be a ride. I showed my good manners by running, hoping that I was not making a fool of myself chasing after a driver who had just stopped to read a map or check his tires. That has happened a few times, and it is embarrassing for both of us. I guess my dubiousness was obvious, because when I opened the passenger door the driver nodded impatiently and said, "Yeah, yeah. Get in."

Another Russian, but younger than Sergei, with shoulder-length blond hair held back by a black macramé headband. He was headed to Portland. As I stowed my stuff, I noticed a guitar tucked behind my seat. "You play guitar?" This time I was asking the stupid question.

"Yes, me and my wife, we have a group. We have four CDs; two CDs her, two CDs me."

"You sing in Russian?"

"Yes of course. Also we have two songs in English."

His English was better than Sergei's, but not as good as Martina's. He came from Moldavia, he told me, "on the Black Sea, near Bulgaria and Romania," and he had been in the United States for about a year and a half. Unlike my other Eastern Europeans, he had been a professional driver back home, though there he had driven buses rather than trucks. Judging by his example, Russian buses must be a good deal more exciting than Trailways or Greyhound. We were heavily loaded—he told me he was hauling 70,000 pounds, though he never said what it was—but he took all the downhill stretches at full speed, barreling past his more cautious peers with a happily contemptuous shout: "Hah! In Russia, we drive like this!"

He was on his way back from New York, where he had spent a free afternoon in Brighton Beach. It had been his first visit, and he was thrilled. "A million Russians! It was like being in Moscow!" He had a box full of new CDs on the floor beside him, all the latest releases, and spent the next three hours giving me a lesson in Russian pop. He never played any album all the way through; he would just spin a song or two, passing me the cover and translating some phrases, then skip to something else. It was a curious mix of styles: The women tended to sound like French chanteuses, post-Piaf power-balladeers with synthesized string sections, while the men growled like Tom Waits, only gruffer and deeper. Two CDs were compilations of Russian Mafia songs, apparently a popular genre. He translated lyrics here and there, a woman singing about how she was born in prison, and men about their money and their power to silence anyone who messed with them. Then came an anthology of comic truck-driving songs, complete with honking horns, roaring engines, and police sirens.

Some of the discs were Russian imports, but at least half had been recorded in New York or Western Europe. The driver's favorite singer—I never managed to catch her name—had been a star in Russia since the 1980s, but now lives in New York. Another, Tatiana somebody, had a new hit aimed specifically at the emigrant audience, which he especially liked and played for me twice, translating the words: "We are all Russians still. Some of us are in New York, Paris, or Berlin, but we are still *ruskya* . . ."

The music notwithstanding, my driver was very pleased to be in the United States. "We were always taught about America, that everything was very bad. We hear this in the school: 'America bad.' Even there was a kind of chewing gum from America, it cost only fifteen kopecks, and some people got cancer and they said it was because of the American chewing gum."

I said that we had heard a lot of the same sorts of things about Russia; that each of our countries had filled people with some pretty bizarre ideas about the other.

"But it is different: Russia is bad. Russia, in this time, you say anything, there are people listening and you can go to jail. You just say, 'I think America is good,' and you can be in jail your whole life."

He was quite a change from Sergei. I wondered if it made a difference that he was younger, or that he had come over with a wife and no children, so had fewer ties to the old country. He was also working harder on his English, asking me to translate signs he did not understand. We passed one saying Deer Crossing, and he asked me, "What is deer?" I did my best deer imitation, stretching up my fingers alongside my head like antlers. He laughed, and nodded, "I understand, OK." An hour or so later we passed a deer, standing a few yards from the road and nervously watching the traffic. He pointed to it, with a big smile, and said, "Ah: deer!" He had tried to find steady work in Portland so that he could take language classes, but the first job he landed was in a carpentry shop and involved so much heavy lifting that he got a hernia and ended up in the hospital—his one criticism of America was the high cost of medical care.

It was dark by the time we passed Pendleton, the last big town before Hermiston and the Seattle turnoff. By then, a steady, cold rain was falling. There were lots of motels lining the highway, and for a moment I considered asking him to let me off right there, but Hermiston seemed like it would be a better place to start in the morning, so I kept my mouth shut and watched the water run down the windows. It was a good night to be indoors.

Another thirty miles, and the signs for Hermiston came up, with a half-dozen motels listed. I told the driver I would stop there, and he said no problem, he wanted to pull over anyway for coffee. Good thing, too, since when we got to the bottom of the exit ramp the signs were more specific, and it turned out that the nearest of the motels was over five miles away, presumably in Hermiston itself. That would be over an hour's walk, in the rain and cold. "So, no problem," my driver said. "You come on to Portland. There is a motel right there on I-5, and tomorrow you go straight to Seattle."

In for a penny, in for a pound. I hadn't been to Portland in twenty years, and might as well spend a night or two there. Meanwhile, I would be warm and dry for another three hours. The only problem was that by now I was utterly exhausted, but there was a solution for that as well. I asked the driver if I could stretch out in back and get a little sleep. I had never made that request before, but Sergei's hospitality had planted the idea in my head, and if my host had any misgivings he was too polite to mention them. So I climbed over my pack, tipped my guitar against the back wall, and lay on the bed, listening to the rain, the motor, and the Russian pop songs, and soon was fast asleep.

DARK STREETS

I woke as we pulled off the highway, about twenty miles outside of Portland. The driver wanted to phone ahead and get directions for his morning delivery, but no one was answering, so we got back on I-84 and I counted down to Exit 1. Luckily for me, Portland is one of the few major cities where the main highway interchange is right in the middle of town. Were I a resident, I suppose I would prefer to have more of the traffic steered around the outskirts, but for once the traffic planners seem to have designed a road system with hitchhikers in mind.

So there I was, just thirty-six hours after leaving Iowa City, already on the West Coast. It hadn't been a particularly distinctive run, but it sure proved the efficacy of the thumb in modern America. A bus wouldn't have come close to that time, and I would have been aching and miserable after just a few hours crammed into the narrow seats. Plus, I would not have met anyone or been given a free course in Czech bluegrass and Russian Mafia songs. The couple of hours of sleep had revived me, and I felt wide awake, full of energy, and ready to see what Portland had to offer.

Walking up the ramp from the interstate, I found myself in a square as blankly deserted as a moonscape. Not a car passed, much less a human being who might give me directions. There was a trolley line, though, and once I figured out which side was signed for downtown, I walked along the tracks.

It was midnight, but I felt safe and at home. The whole trip had been a linked chain of lucky chances, and Portland has always been a hospitable town for tramps and hoboes. It was a stronghold of the Industrial Workers of the World, America's most freewheeling labor union, and the "Wobblies" staged their most famous free speech fight here, protesting a local ordinance against "radical" orators by calling in hundreds of migrant loggers and farmworkers to stand on soapboxes and get hauled off by the cops, until the jails were full and the law had to be repealed as unenforceable. That was almost a century ago, but a lot of the downtown feels as if it hasn't changed. There are new buildings, but also the fleabag hotels and greasy diners that once could be reliably found near any urban center. "Skid row" was a Portland invention, named for the blocks of saloons and flophouses along which drunken loggers reeled like felled trees "skidded" on greased planks, and today it is a precious relic of more convivial times. Most American cities have urban-renewed their transient districts out of existence, and now the only cheap places to stay are motels by the highway exits—handy enough if you've got a car, but unhelpful for travelers without vehicles or a lot of money. Which, of course, is one reason why the cities destroyed the old districts. Anyway, I remembered Portland's skid row fondly, and was looking forward to its seedy hospitality. All I had to do was figure out how to get there from where I was.

Ten minutes down the trolley line, a lighted platform solved the problem. Two guys were loitering listlessly on my side of the tracks, smoking cigarettes and looking like they planned to stay the night. A third man sat on the other side, cross-legged on the concrete, whittling on a walking stick. He was buried in his work, and pointedly ignoring the others, so I approached them first. Did they know where I could find a cheap bed for the night? One of them, a small, dark guy with curly hair and red eyes, suggested I try a motel on Burnside, a couple of blocks over, he thought it was about forty dollars. Not too promising, but I had nothing to lose by checking it out. He was mumbling directions when the guy across the way said, "It's better downtown."

The guy I was talking with said, "Downtown there are roaches."

"No. On Stark Street."

"Oh, yeah, maybe. But that's a long way."

"It's not so far." The whittler got up and put his knife in his pocket. "Look, I'll walk you down there."

It sounded like the right area, or at least a better bet than where I was. I thanked the dark guy and his friend, who had stood silently nodding agreement throughout the conversation. "Please, I'm mentally ill," the dark guy mumbled, by way of farewell. "I'm sleeping on the street. Could you give me some change?"

I gave him a buck for luck, then had to run to catch up with my guide, who was walking quickly down the tracks without looking back. He glanced at me when I came alongside, but said nothing, and kept his brisk pace. He was pale and blond, with hair below his shoulders and a straight, pointed beard. He was wearing old, faded jeans, hiking boots, a gray, hooded wool sweater, and a battered brown felt hat. About my height and build, and a fast walker.

We continued along the trolley line, passing another station or two, then turned left. There was a bridge ahead, a bizarre steel structure looming in the darkness. It looked like something out of a gothic fairy tale: two tall black towers supporting a sort of house suspended in the air. I couldn't make it out clearly, but I suppose it must have been some sort of elevator system to raise the center of the bridge when ships came through. It looked ancient and ominous, an ogre's castle of the industrial age. On the right, below us as we mounted the bridge, was an immense cement grain elevator, towering white in the moonlight, with a thin building running on tracks along its upper wall on the river side, presumably to feed the grain into the ships' holds. It had that strange poetry of stone and metal, an awesome structure that could be strikingly ugly or beautiful depending on the light and your mood. I suppose that back when Notre Dame was being built, there were old folks clucking their tongues at the ugliness of modern technology, and murmuring about how much prettier thatch was than stone. I had grown up lamenting the ugliness of big, industrial monstrosities in my hometown, while meanwhile learning Woody Guthrie's Columbia River ballads, celebrating the Grand Coulee Dam and the industry that now surrounded me. I was crossing his "sandy Willamette," with the Columbia just a couple of miles north, and that grain elevator is there to ensure that his "shiploads of plenty will steam past the locks." The steam is gone, but I have no reason to think he would have missed it. Woody was not a nostalgic man. And, for those who are, it is worth considering that time eventually hallows everything. As Maxwell Anderson wrote, back in the 1930s, "Nothing is made by man but makes, in the end, good ruins."

Stepping onto the bridge, the steel walkway clanged under our feet and the first tower arched ahead like the gates of hell. My Virgil walked silently beside me. It was a perfect welcome to Portland, the lights of the town glittering ahead, the sound of the water below. I had no idea where we were or where we were headed, and this seemed a good moment to orient myself. Breaking the silence, I asked, "Which way is the center of town?"

My guide stopped and gestured. "Dead ahead. You see those tall buildings? We're coming out of East Portland into West Portland." He swept his right hand along, as if following a line of streets: "The streets running across there are all the numbered streets, and then the way we're walking are all the lettered streets, Burnside, Couch, Davis, Everett . . ." His hand paralleled each street as he said the name, coming down along it like a karate chop. He talked as quickly as he had walked, and never looked at me, only at the streets and buildings ahead.

At least he was talking. "Are you from here?" I asked.

"I grew up in Portland. I was in central Oregon for a while, but I had to come back here to go to jail." He was walking again, his eyes on the sidewalk in front of his feet, but the ice had been broken. "Where are you coming in from?"

"I just hitched in from Boston."

"I used to live out there, in Lowell. I liked it there. I went out there with my girlfriend. But that's where I got into dope. We drove all over the country, had a van all set up to sleep in. We went to Mexico, everyplace, and then up the East Coast. We ended up in Lowell. It was a good place to live. A lot of Spanish people. But then I got strung out, and ended up back in Oregon. I got straightened out in prison, but now I'm on the street and I got strung out all over again."

He asked where I was headed, and I said Vancouver.

"Vancouver, Washington, or BC?"

"Canada."

"That's smart. I hear it's a lot more liberal up there. Down here it's so stupid. Tobacco and alcohol are legal, and they bust you for dope. And the worst drugs are legal."

At the end of the bridge we turned left and walked down a bigger street, past a couple of bars that were closing for the night, the last customers drifting out to their cars. We turned right, then left again. At the corner there was a little open area in front of an office building, and my guide stopped and began giving me directions toward Stark, then cut himself off with a shake of his head. "I'll just walk you over there. I'm coming back here to sleep, but you don't want to get lost." I said it seemed like kind of sketchy weather for sleeping out, but he said it was all right, he knew a good place.

We turned right on Stark, and he began pointing out landmarks: Powell's Bookstore was down to the right, and that glowing sign was the Clyde Hotel, one of the oldest in Portland. It was an ornate beacon of old neon, and the hotel looked like something from Jack London's day. Up another block I could find the Roxy, an all-night diner, where they gave you a whole thermos of coffee for a buck. "I'm sorry, I don't know how you're set, but if you could give me a dollar that would be great. I didn't plan to ask you, I wasn't thinking about that. But it just crossed my mind now."

I said I'd be happy to give him five, and many thanks. We had been walking for half an hour, and I would never have found this neighborhood on my own. I didn't have anything but a couple of twenties, though, so when we reached the hotel he had in mind I went in to get change. The hotel was called the Joyce, with a sign on the door advertising rooms for twenty-two dollars, twenty-seven dollars with television, or fourteen dollars for just a bed and a locker. My guide squatted on the sidewalk beside the door while I went inside. The clerk was locked away behind bulletproof glass. He said he had a room free, but he couldn't give me change until I finished checking in and paying. I started doing the paperwork, and meanwhile a cop car pulled up in front and called my friend over. I started out the door to tell them he had been helping me, that he wasn't just loitering on the street, but they were simply checking him out and he was handling it all calmly, so I went back inside and waited while the clerk wrote down my license number, filled out my name and room in the ledger book, and counted my change. Then I paid my guide, said good-bye, and headed upstairs for a long, hot shower and a decent night's sleep.

AND THE GODS LAUGHED

awoke to the sound of a torrential rainstorm. It was Monday, the museums were closed, and my only friends in Portland were out of town, so I decided I might as well catch a train up to Seattle. Much as I love hitchhiking, the routes out of Portland and into Seattle are mazes of crisscrossing interstates, and what with the rain it didn't seem to make sense to spend the next few hours soaking myself on a succession of suburban on-ramps.

So I abandoned the road for that one leg of the journey, and the gods were quick to punish my transgression: when my train was a half hour out of Portland, a car veered off the highway into a utility pole and dragged a tangle of high-tension power cables down onto the track just as the locomotive got to where it couldn't stop without hitting them. We had cables under the wheels and more cables strung out along the roof, and all of them were live and could not be touched until the electric company sent a truck out. So there we sat for the next five hours, watching the accident get cleared away, then the cars and semis driving smoothly on toward Seattle under what was now a clear, blue sky.

Of course, the highway gods are just a gambler's superstition, forgotten as soon as I get off the road, but this time it was hard not to think that they were really up there messing with me. I was making a hitchhiking trip I hoped to turn into a book, and had slipped and taken one little train, and suddenly there was a disaster that backed up traffic for a dozen miles and stranded me with nothing to do but buy a bland sandwich in the dining car and curse my sorry fate—not to mention the fate of the poor guy who hit the telephone pole. It certainly felt as if some twenty-first-century Olympians were amusing themselves at my expense. Or maybe I misunderstood the message, and they were just trying to provide me with a flashy ending.

In any case, the accident drove home the lesson I had set out to illustrate: you travel best when you trust your luck and the folks you meet along the road. It's not a complicated lesson, but it has to be learned over and over again. The train, bus, and airline schedules keep promising reliable arrivals at fixed times and places, and as we get older the temptation only grows to buy our tickets and find our places in the orderly rows of identical seats. But trains, planes, and buses break down, crash, or get delayed—sometimes entire lines go out of business, leaving thousands of people unexpectedly stranded—and they often are slow and uncomfortable even when they arrive as promised. So, for some of us at least, it's a perfectly sensible choice to take our chances, sit up front beside the driver, chat for an hour or two, and trust that when this ride ends another one will come along.

The lifestyle metaphor is clear, but I also am talking about real roads and real drivers. I would like to see a lot more young people out on the highway, thumbs in the air, showing their optimism and faith in the world around them. Especially here in the United States. This trip reminded me how much I love the wide expanses of this country, and its inexhaustible variety of land and people. Americans are getting stereotyped as violent and paranoid, even by ourselves, and it is a relief to be reminded how many of us are helpful and friendly, ready to interrupt our daily rounds at the solicitation of a random wanderer.

This trip went by more quickly than I expected, but that just proves that hitchhiking is still an excellent way to travel. So this is not an end of any kind, just an appetizer for future, more ambitious journeys. I have dreamed for many years of making a full-length hitch of the Americas, from Alaska to Tierra del Fuego. The tricky part will be the Darien Gap, between Panama and Colombia—a swampy jungle that was hard to cross even before it became a center of guerrilla warfare and drug trafficking—but in dangerous terrain, there is no better place to be than on the side of the road with your thumb in the air. You may look odd and naïve, but you don't look like a rich tourist, a drug smuggler, or a government agent. And if the overland route is impassable, I can stick my thumb out on the coast—there are people who do all their hitchhiking on boats, and it's about time I gave that a try. There is a big world out there, full of all kinds of roads—and everywhere, there are strangers who will become friends as soon as they pull over.

ENVOI: MEXICO 1987

A dusty wind took me two hundred miles,
Through mountains with sharp corners, ragged grass,
And little towns where girls in city styles
Watched Sunday soccer after morning mass.
On steel truck-beds like silver wings I rode
And froze the views like flowers held in glass,
Ahead the hills like solemn sentries stood,
Then parted silently to let me pass.
When I am eighty, let it be the same,
Still on the road, the highway flying by,
No family, no fortune and no fame,
But wind, and dusty roads, and open sky.
And seeking something just around the bend—
Not finding, only seeking till the end.